More praise for
I'll Have Some of Yours

"As a health care professional dedicated to exemplary dementia care, I was moved by Annette's story and experience as a family caregiver. While every story is unique—like every individual and family on this journey—Annette captures the complex emotions common to many families faced with this disease. Her book is a touching personal narrative and example of unwavering commitment and love of family."

> – Susan Gilster, PhD, RN, Gilster and Associates.
> Alois Alzheimer Center, founder, operator, 1987-2012

"As a professional working in the dementia field, I found that "I'll Have Some of Yours" beautifully captures the hidden joys that Annette discovers through her mother's life lessons."

> – Kristin Cooley, LISW-S, LCSW

"Annette Januzzi Wick takes us on a bittersweet journey with her mother sharing stories that show the miraculous power of music to impact the lives of those with dementia."

> – Wayne "Woody" Mesker, Musician, Director of Outreach,
> Alive Inside Foundation, founder, Rock Against Dementia

I'll Have Some of Yours

I'll Have Some of Yours

What I learned from my mother
about dementia, cookies, music, the outside,
and her life inside a care home.

Annette Januzzi Wick

THREE
ARCH PRESS

Author's Note: Some names and locations were
changed to protect the privacy of the dear ones I
befriended. The mistakes—and the memories—are mine.

FIRST EDITION

Library of Congress Control Number: 2019904555

ISBN – 978-0-9774856-1-1

Cover Design: Elaine Olund
Layout Design: Lauren Whaley

Printed in the United States of America on acid-free paper.

1 2 3 4 5 6 7 8 9 10

For Mom

Contents

Jean, we try to spare our kids so much pain
but I guess we have to let them experience that pain
and that is the way they learn
and remember the experience.

– Mary Jane Berens, in a letter to my mother.

Prologue

I'LL HAVE SOME OF YOURS

In which I learn why my mother ate half my sandwich.

I grew up in a boisterous and moody Italian household where my mother executed banquets of rolled antipasti, fresh ravioli, wedding soup, and trays of Italian cookies with the precision of a five-star restaurant chef.

Leftovers were prized possessions.

If I crept into the kitchen late at night, made a sandwich with crusty Italian bread from a cousin's bakery, and layered it with capicola, prosciutto, and the hard kind of provolone that caused my teeth to tingle, the rattling of silverware in the drawer beckoned my mother from her chair as she dozed in the nearby family room. She didn't plan to miss out on enjoying all the remnants of her hard work. "Oh boy, that looks good," she said. Her brown eyes, as circular as her round face, grew into huge ovals as she surveyed my sandwich piled high. I asked if she wanted me to fix her something too.

Slyly and smartly, she said, "No, thanks. I'll have some of yours."

Back then, I thought *I'll have some of yours* was my mother's way of saying, "I'm tired. I did all the work, now I'll just borrow from you and have some of what's on your plate."

But she wasn't just talking about the sandwich when she said that line. As my mother fried Canadian bacon during the Sunday brunch feasts she cooked for my visiting college roommates, listened to me griping about why my high school English teacher didn't like my work, held my words in letters I wrote home when my thirty-eight-year-old husband was diagnosed with cancer, or baked and brought cookies to my young, teething son—cookies that were a sign of her generosity and constancy—she meant,

"I'll take some of that burden off of you and put it on me."

Then, dementia took a seat beside me at my mother's cherished oval table.

The mother who gave birth to me after my father drove to the hospital in a blinding January snowstorm was no longer the woman in front of me.

As her caregiver, I daily swooped into her care home and we leisurely walked along the corridors or lingered outside in the courtyard. Yet there were times I found myself rushing to the ER of a hospital, my heart banging, determined to do anything to hold onto her physically. I was her bodyguard and her safety net. If I could protect her from a fall by making her walk more or keep her from contracting the flu, she wouldn't lose more of her memory and I could keep alive the mother who had given me life and loved me as her daughter. And I could protect myself from feeling her loss…or so I hoped.

I know this now: When I stopped changing what I thought should be changed—combing my mother's hair constantly, making her bed perfectly, neatly rearranging her clothes in the closet after the staff washed them— and was quiet enough to listen to her breathe, I relieved her of my expectation to still be Mom to me. I could enjoy her as a woman who no longer knew my name but knew she loved me and wanted to press her head into the crook of my neck as we sat in the sun together or shared food from a single dish.

In her final months, my mother still scrounged off my plate that held mini-cupcakes, squares of cheese, or flattened blackberries. But she wasn't only borrowing food, she was borrowing the memories she had lost. Fish sticks reminded her of Lenten Fish Fries at our family's parish of St. Joseph's. Chocolate-covered caramels reminded her of the box of Faroh's pecan turtles my father gave her every birthday, anniversary and any holiday in between.

With her fingers or a fork, she slid my food in her mouth and offered up an inscrutable smile—a smile as wide as a tomato that reminded me of summer and canning jars and youth. Then came the line that always followed her smile:

"I'll have some of yours," she would say, picking up half-eaten pizza crusts or homegrown cucumber slices on my plate and stuffing them in her mouth.

Looking back now, after my mother's death, what I remember most was how the mother in front of me became the woman I loved…and I miss her.

I miss her eating from my plate, or yelling at me, a part of my daily routine as much as brushing my teeth. I never thought I would miss that person who couldn't live on her own, was often silent, or sleeping, or saying something derogatory about me or anyone else around me (except for my husband because she adored his sparkling blue eyes). I never thought I would miss someone who was already missing so much. But I do.

Mostly, I miss my mother's touch, a touch that can't be pressed into a photo album, a touch I still feel…as if I have a phantom hand holding mine. Touch was what mattered most between us. When her fingers squeezed at my cheeks, when we held each other up as we walked or our bodies embraced in a hug, the pain we both experienced—of the sameness of her days, of the loneliness in a woman who had never met a stranger and then only saw strangers daily in her life—disappeared.

All that mattered—other than cookies we piled up on a plate and ate together —was the way our lives became one life shared when we sat side by side at her care home, gazing out across the grass, mostly at a white wooden fence and the scampering squirrels. We scooted toward each other and made the separation between us smaller, thinner, even invisible.

Finally, we drove away the pain, climbed inside each other's hearts and said, "I'll have some of your love and you can have some of mine."

Mom Needs
a Different Home

In which I learn to take baby steps.

My aging parents stood on opposite sides of sliding glass doors leading to an old sandstone building now used as a skilled rehab center. My eighty-two-year-old mother, Jean, short and mighty, planted her feet on the rubber mat. "I'm not going in." She demanded my father, Ette (pronounced *Eh-tee*), who stood at the same height as her, drive her home. She had just come out of surgery and was instructed to spend two weeks in rehab to heal.

"Okay, Jean," my father said, running hands over his head where gray hairs hung on. He did as he was told and drove her home.

After being at her side for the operation, I had already left town and was furious when I found out what he'd done.

My mother had begun to forget calendar appointments, doctors' orders, the names of her grandchildren. After she underwent surgery for her abdominal swelling and was released, recovery was not the only issue. The size and the emptiness of their home, as well as her care, were also problems. How could he take her home? But he did.

My parents lived in the same two-story colonial-style house close to their hometown of Lorain for over thirty years. Their soaring house was once festooned outside with *Peace on Earth* spelled out in Christmas lights along the back fence separating our yard from the highway. Inside, five children clamored for attention and the bathroom. But not anymore.

Given my father's willingness to cave in to *the boss*, as he called my mother, they were now without clear oversight and a clearer plan. Some of their grown children lived out of town, like me, or worked to balance families and jobs. I was four years into a new marriage after the death of my first husband, and had three stepdaughters who joined my young son. I visited my parents less and the number of children or grandchildren in the home shrank.

Surely, my parents had conversations about their long-term physical and mental health needs, I convinced myself. My father, a former business owner who staked every tomato plant at the same height, and my mother, who haunted every speck of dust that haunted her, dutifully completed Health Care Power of Attorney forms and Advanced Directives. I coerced them into filling out Vial of Life forms for emergency situations, and like a proud parent, hung the papers on their refrigerator door with the Tillamook Ice Cream magnet next to the cheeky smiles of toddler granddaughters who had the same bright, brown Italian eyes as their ancestors. I thought it was a good start. Now, I had documentation for which of my father's kidneys had been removed and which breast my mother lost. In that same session, we never addressed whether they had to move—and when.

I badgered my father across the miles of telephone wire spanning from Cincinnati to northern Ohio. "I can't believe you let Mom talk you into her not going to rehab and took her home instead. She can't get what she needs at home." How could I tell him, a man who had given everything to his family, that my mother's needs were now beyond what any one person could offer? My father couldn't do it alone and shouldn't want to try.

As adults, though maybe not in our parents' eyes, all of us children made phone calls and outright pleas for my father to admit he needed assistance. My youngest sister, Jeanne, lived nearby and had been dutifully on standby for years, but even she couldn't maintain that position forever. "We'll pay for it," I offered, knowing money was at the heart of some things that mattered to him. We were willing to pay for a cleaning person, someone to mow the **damn grass** (as my mother called the half acre of green), rake the leaves that fell from the three silver maple trees. Someone, anyone. I lived four hours away by car—I couldn't offer myself.

"I don't want strangers in here," my father said gruffly into the brown desk phone, in the stubborn tradition associated with his generation and Italian background. I imagined him sitting in his den, surrounded by his former lives of shoe store proprietor and real estate agent. "We have lots of valuables. My stamp collection. Your mother's Lladro figures. Someone'll walk off with them. I don't want anyone else in my business."

For weeks, my four siblings and I lobbed comments and suggestions toward my father. For weeks, he tossed them aside. He played the role of martyr to one child—*What do you want me to do?*—and the role of strong dictator to the next—*I won't do it.* I often hung up the phone confused. Had I spoken to Jekyll or Hyde?

My father's short black locks had thinned and grayed over the years, coiling mostly around his lower head to keep his ears warm. I didn't know what raw emotion or information couldn't get through his head—or weakened heart valves. Over the phone, I couldn't see how his love for my mother and the shame of not being able to care for his wife might also cause him to fear the unknown. I did, however, possess the background of tending to my first husband, Devin, through his cancer diagnosis and death. I still regretted that in Devin's death, I gave more care than I did love, because that was what was required. *Do you understand that, Dad?* Here I was, the daughter, counseling him against making the same mistake I had made.

Perhaps my father felt it was his duty to provide care for his wife in the way of food, clothing and shelter. And this he was doing.

The night before my mother's operation, I had slept in the sunny yellow bedroom of my youth in my parents' home. In the age-old tradition of foraging through the kitchen for leftovers, I smelled something foul and found a roast of turkey turned blue, rotting in the refrigerator. Dish towels were left unwashed and stiff. Baggies from store-bought cold cuts were being reused to store wedges of Romano cheese. My parents must have thought salmonella had been eradicated.

And, as I told my father, "I think Mom is lonely and she could use a hair wash."

My mother once maintained a pristine home with carpeting fibers in every room standing at attention, and an unspoiled personal appearance where not a brown or graying hair lay out of place. Like my father, she was of her generation. She took pride in what little she could control. Before we had driven to the hospital for her operation, she halted progress at the hallway mirror to swipe on some muted red color of lipstick. And throughout her stay, she kept asking, "Where is my comb?" She looked for her flimsy comb in the plastic bin, the nightstand and her sheets.

During our time waiting in the hard, vinyl chairs of the hospital, my father and I, surrounded by the scents of sterility and reality, grunted at her incessant questions. *Where am I? What is this?*

My father had looked at me with sunken brown eyes. "I should have taken your mother on more vacations." Adventuresome before marriage, my mother always wanted to travel. Over the years, she arranged family outings to center around warm temperatures, while my father pushed for more historical context in our trips. But in their later years, he preferred to stay at home, watching his pennies or his garden.

At first, I trembled at his admission. Then I'd wondered if my father's comment was a sign he saw the future. He was ready to take that first step—admitting there was a problem.

But later, he'd allowed my mother to walk out of therapy critical to her healing. Of course, she, too, was of an obstinate, Italian ancestry and plotted out her day with the same vision as she plotted tasks in the kitchen. She was hard to cross.

Now, following my mother's surgery, my father was trapped. At home, she forgot her ravaged body could not hold weight and lifted overflowing laundry baskets and grocery bags of flour and sugar. "At least she's doing the laundry," he said when I blew up at him over the phone, fast becoming a habit of mine. He balked again at additional help, giving more of his tired lines. "I don't want new people in the house. They'll scare your mother."

"But what would scare her more? A house on fire? An unrecognizable home? A move?" I hadn't meant to throw out a threat, so I softened. "These caregivers could also become friends." My mother was a friend gatherer, the first link in a phone chain, the first to drop a get-well card in the mail. She was a person who needed people. And she could use a friend to return the favor, one who might not fear her as she retreated to the corners of her mind, unlike her children who pressured her into doing what we wanted.

"Remember what you said about vacations, Dad? I doubt Mom will be going on too many more, but she can still retain some dignity." I didn't know how much he really respected my opinions, as we hadn't been close since I moved away after college. But I felt it was my duty to lobby for my mother. My past role as advocate for Devin might not have persuaded my father to act, but it had taught me to be the voice for decency. "And she could still have a clean home and good hair," I added as a joke.

My father and I made a deal.

He would concede. So would I.

My father yielded long enough for a woman named Tamara to visit and sit with my mother. He and I did not talk in detail about the situation. I didn't want to open the door for him to picket our pact.

One morning, I called home. Tamara answered and said that my father had just left for a meeting. In the background, I heard my mother laughing as she came to the phone. "Hi, Mom. What are you up to?"

"Oh. Hi, 'Net."

For years, my mother had called me 'Net and, to my father, I was 'Net Marie. According to her, she gave her children names that could not be shortened. But Annette did lend itself to nicknames. And for years, I'd endured monikers and mispronunciations such as Nettie, Netti Spaghetti, Annie, Anita, or Janette, until one day I discovered my great-grandmother had been named *Annatonia*. I longed to be that woman instead, one with an Italian name, though *Annatonia* and *Annette* were rather close in sound.

My knees weakened at the sound of my nickname. It had taken forty years for me find out I didn't need to be Annette, or Annatonia. Suddenly, I was thrilled to be 'Net to her, to hear the lightness in her voice.

"I have a friend here," my mother continued. "And we're going to sit outside. It's so beautiful today."

"Yeah? What's it like?"

"Colors. And sun."

Living over two hundred miles away in Cincinnati, I imagined a similar fall day to the one I was experiencing while gazing out the sliding glass door of my kitchen into the stand of cottonwood trees, a crisp apple smell detected in the wash of red and orange leaves floating through the air. I puffed up my chest, hearing my mother smile in her declaration.

We didn't speak at length. I wanted her to hold fast to that sense of friendship and freedom and sunshine. I hung up and cried a little, called my youngest sister to relay the story and sobbed again.

We were all taking baby steps.

"SOMETIMES I THINK I HAVE THAT DISEASE... WHAT DO THEY CALL IT?"

In which I convince my father to start talking — about talking.

"Ette, are you there?" my mother asked in a stern voice, using my father's nickname. "You can say something too." She, my father and I were engaged in a three-way phone conversation diagonally across the state of Ohio.

"I can come home Tuesday," I offered. "Tuesday night, I can drive up—"

"Ette, you have a dentist appointment on Tuesday. Will you have time to see the barber for a haircut?" Reading off the calendar in front of her while seated at her Formica kitchen desk, my mother spoke over me. "Ette, did you hear me?"

"Jean, didn't you hear your daughter?" my father asked, muttering from the phone in his office two rooms away from her. According to my father, I was always **your** daughter (they had four), and my mother was **your** mother. "She wants to come visit on Tuesday."

"Who wants to come Tuesday?" my mother asked.

I broke in. "Me, Mom. Annette." I didn't have time for this. I didn't need permission to come home, did I? I was simply letting them know.

"Ette, I see on my calendar you have…"

I heard my father sigh. I sighed too. My mother had become forgetful, and relentless in her forgetfulness.

Telephone calls to my parents were a constant source of my entertainment…and frustration. The content was an interweaving of my father's silences or brief commentaries on the highway patrol and those damn politicians, and my mother's recitations about church feast days and protestations of anything related to Dad.

My mother had always been the primary communicator and caregiver in the family. As a former first-grade teacher, she was our source for organization, too. Seated at her desk in the kitchen, surrounded by piles of bills in envelopes with due dates written neatly in her handwriting, she pored over AAA books, folded the corners of the pages of Florida hotels suitable for a family of seven (two double beds and space for three sleeping bags in one room) and familiarized herself with the rest stops in each TripTik acquired. Every night, she mapped out family dinners in her kitchen like a military officer in battle. When the troops diminished, she still managed to press out a pot of tomato sauce and roll around dozens of meatballs, creating mouth-watering smells I could almost breathe in over the phone.

During evenings in my childhood, following parties and celebrations, we kids readily excused ourselves and went to bed while our parents stood at the sink, drying the dishes my mother refused to let air-dry. To my father's dismay, he would be allowed to turn in only when all the party platters were back in place.

Raised for a time by a single mother when her birth father died, my mother never did allow for life to be left to its own devices.

Even during her breast cancer surgery and a hip replacement procedure, she had defined the phrase *taking care of everything*, including over the phone.

But those three-way calls had turned into four. Like the switchboard operator waiting for a call to finish, my mother's dementia had become a party on the line.

My father became the primary communicator but he didn't relish the role. "Hallo," he answered the next time I called.

"Hey, Dad. What's going on today?" I was in the car, driving to pick up my son, Davis, from baseball practice.

"Hold on before I get too far. Let me get your mother on the line," he said, his tone hesitant.

I breathed. I didn't know if I had the patience for another round of "Who's on First?" Maybe he didn't either.

My mother eased in a "Hello," and giggled while she mentioned the temperature. "Oh, it's cold here today. Right, Ette? What's it doing…where you live?" she asked, tentative about which child she was speaking to in which location.

"In Cincinnati," I said to help her along. Of course, I was one of two daughters in that city.

She said nothing more and disappeared into the background fizzing of the phone line.

In my teens, when one of my sisters had called my mother and unceasingly discussed her dilemma of the day, I'd watched my mother hold the phone away from her reddening ear. Sometimes, the calls were hours' long.

I was envious of my sisters then. I wasn't a phone talker, nor was my life exciting enough to reach the same animated levels that my sisters' lives achieved.

Now, to my mother, three minutes on the phone felt like twenty-four hours. She had participated in a lifetime of phone conversations, times five. She didn't need any more fuss to fill her headspace. She had torments of her own to wrestle, moving the church bulletin from one pile to another, only to search for it again to be certain she hadn't missed Mass.

As my mother vacated the conversation, my father gave a slight chuckle. In his husky voice that hid it all so well, he asked, "Well, 'Net Marie, what are you gonna do?"

She no longer was obliged to listen to any us, including my father.

"Anyhow," he went on, "we gotta get to the doctor's."

Keeper of that secret life inside my mother's head, he also became keeper of the desk calendar produced by the church. My parents visited their doctors more than their children, not necessarily by choice. He scribbled a myriad of doctor and clinical appointments in his hieroglyphic handwriting on the calendar, spelled out alongside Holy Days of Obligation: cardiologist – his; gynecologist – hers; neurologist – his; eye doctor – hers. Juxtaposed were my mother's handwritten notations of birthdays, anniversaries and deaths. Our lives had been interwoven with those of the Catholic saints.

My mother jumped back on the line again. "Ette, who are you talking to?" she asked with all the innocence of a three-year-old wanting attention.

I didn't know what to say for a moment. Then I continued with our conversation. "Wow, Dad. Doctor visits occupy all your time these days," I said, ignoring my mother, but immediately wanting to take back my judgment against my father. They weren't avoiding the inevitable, just not sharing it with me.

"Oh, no," he said, drawing out *oh*. "We're not at that stage yet. We just have one appointment today."

"Ette, what appointment, what are you…" In the midst of my mother asking, she forgot her flow of words. "Oh damn it. Sometimes I think I have that disease…What do they call it?"

I knew what they called it. I started to feel its presence. But, like the rest of my family, I refused to name it.

Our phone conversations became snippets of dialogue with less weight and more gravitas.

My father did not rise to the role of the great communicator or compassionate caregiver willingly. He was drafted and came mostly kicking and screaming. He grit his teeth while I convinced him it was time to switch his wife over to the care of a gerontologist, away from the convenience offered by the family doctor (Dr. X) down the street. He occasionally said, *I go see Dr. X, just for some things.* I couldn't blame him for wanting familiarity. He presently slept with a wife who was having trouble remembering to make the bed. Even the sherbet-green bedspread was becoming unfamiliar to her.

One day, my father phoned. His voice faltered as I picked up the call. "I'm having a hard time, 'Net Marie, leaving the house with your mother for groceries. She wanders in the store and asks a million questions and wants to leave before we pay."

The predicaments continued. "I left the house for my housing authority meeting and she didn't remember where I was. She called the cell phone eight times. Eight times."

He discovered napkins and dish cloths stashed in closets with sweaters and jackets. He couldn't locate the keys to the Chevy Blazer and *Your mother doesn't know where she left them.* The missing keys were the least of the worries when it came to her driving. But soon, she stopped driving altogether, commanded by a fear far greater than the insurance company.

For a while, I kept my mouth shut. My father didn't want to hear my tirade.

Puzzled by my silence, his voice dropped in sorrow. "Well, 'Net Marie, what am I gonna do? Your mother is the only one I have left to talk to anymore." Like my mother, my father was also eighty-two. Friends of his were dying at the same pace as the juniper bushes around their home. "And she forgets everything I tell her."

In that line, the avalanche of fifty years of marriage rumbled down the mountain and landed on my father's heart.

I bit my tongue. I should have just listened but I couldn't. I wanted to fix the things I couldn't see. "Dad, what about a support group?"

"Yeah, I've been thinking about one." He sounded confident, near resolute.

I perked up. My father now talked about talking. Yet, I didn't know what that actually meant.

My father was silent in a way where his actions showed his love. If he slipped me a five-dollar bill to stop at Wendy's on my commute back to Cincinnati, it meant, *Hey, take care of yourself.* If he drove my car to fill my gas tank while I showered before a long road trip, it meant, *I love you.* He was an action person, not a feelings one. Me too, which was why I continued to push.

"Dad, I saw a therapist…after Devin died. I never told you, but surely you knew, or heard. Or read about it." (The joke in our family was that anything in my life was written in my first published book, *I'll Be in the Car.*) My reminding him could help him open up.

My father was raised by staunch Catholics but now slept in the pews during long sermons. "Why didn't you just go to church and confession?" he asked.

"Confession wouldn't have been enough," I whispered. I was raised in that same religion, a religion that hadn't saved me from nights of sweat and fears. Confession would never have been enough for me. It wouldn't be for him either.

But my father was now talking—about talking.

IT'S NOT ABOUT THE SHOES

In which I see the future in my mother's eyes.

"I don't want anything for Mother's Day—but I do want to be with Mom," I said to my husband and kids over a quick dinner of pancakes before our round of pick-ups and drop-offs with our teenagers.

Mark made an *umhumm* sound while chewing on syrup-soaked pancakes. He was always my ally.

My parents lived half a day away by car. While my husband and I were still obliged to tote kids to college or stay put for other kids to attend school or work, I also wanted to give my father a break from the winter winds of northern Ohio, and from my mother's increasing outbursts that he called daily to report on. It was clear to me my mother's mental capacities continued to decline into a moderate form of dementia. And there was proof. She wasn't cooking for my father. My parents were eating carryout chicken from the convenience store and buying up the entire line of Progresso soups.

It was late when I arrived in our small town—the Sandstone Capital of the World—Amherst, Ohio. The plan was for me to stay one night then bring my parents to Cincinnati for a few days. Both of them waited for me at the door like two little mice peeping out of their hole.

My mother, dressed in her pink duster and faux embroidery slippers, reached out and hugged me. "Oh 'Net, now where did you come from?"

"Cincinnati," I said, and set down my backpack while glancing at the sizeable family activity corkboard where we once had hung report cards and sports banquet programs. Those were gone. And since my previous visit four months earlier, little information had changed other than the rotation of business cards with doctors' appointments.

"That's right. Is that with Mark Manley?" my mother asked, surprising me by using my second husband's name, and squeezing my cheeks with one cold hand, as if she were trying hard to remember something, or me.

I nodded.

Together, we stood in the dim light of the mudroom hallway, me with my puffy coat still on. The sharp scent of winter hung in the air. It was always ten or fifteen degrees colder in northern Ohio from winter through mid-spring. But I was chilled more by the faces I saw, drawn in and tired ones, where once they were alive with smiles when I came to visit.

By now, I had instituted a system of call and responses to allow my mother to remember things without knowing she had forgotten them. I took her arm as we walked into the kitchen. "I live in Cincinnati, with my husband, Mark Manley, and Cheryl, Shannon, Kaitlyn and Davis, and Enzo, our dog."

I glanced back over my shoulder to see my dad cower in the face of a darkness neither of us wanted to name.

"I remember Enzo was little just like this." My mother held her curled hands six inches apart. "Remember. You didn't want that dog. That was **our** dog."

My father, wearing pajamas that were beginning to sag, shook his head in the background.

What I remembered was that my father had wanted the runt from that same litter as Enzo's, of eight Cavalier King Charles Spaniels. But their lifestyle didn't allow for a puppy who could run away at a moment's notice when a door was absentmindedly opened or who could be left in the cold after it closed. Even then, two years earlier, he had sensed my mother's senses were slipping.

I agreed with my mother. It wasn't worth wasting our time together rewiring her memory to note that a few years back she and my father had accompanied me to the breeder's pen outside of Cleveland to wait for a puppy to pick me. Appropriately, Enzo's first night with us was spent in my mother's house. She always saw Enzo as hers.

We woke in the morning, and, in their bedroom, I packed for both of my parents. Well, my father picked out his own clothes while he asked me to dress my mother. I chose a beige top and pants and she slipped them on while I selected a variety of black clothes to pack. I placed her underwear in the suitcase while she stood watch over me, then set her black shoes out to wear.

"Where are we going? What are you doing? I want my brown shoes." She was adamant about wearing her brown wedge shoes—shoes that were too small. Shoes were always a sticking point in a family that had owned a shoe store. I let it go. So much I was learning to do. We were traveling by car and I could encourage her to take off the shoes if they bothered her.

The four-hour ride to Cincinnati was uneventful, except for my mother's predictable complaints about her tight shoes. According to iTunes, we listened to thirty-six Frank Sinatra songs, which kept her mind off her aching feet. My mother sang every line with a yearning in her heart and a soft, warm tone in her voice. I used to wonder if as a teen she had dreamed about Frank the way I once had dreamed about my teenage idol, Bruce Springsteen. Hearing her voice the length of four soundtracks, I had my answer.

Once we settled into my suburban home, I sensed something was out of place for my mother. Like a kid staring into an open refrigerator trying to decide what to eat, she planted her feet on the wood floor and stared out the kitchen window over the ceramic sink. I thought she was watching the squirrels scramble up the feeder post. But she didn't flinch when I came up alongside her. She was lost in thoughts I couldn't access.

In the morning, from the second floor, I heard her rummaging in the kitchen. She knew where the cereal was stored in the pantry, having spent a year's worth of nights with us over time. But she didn't want to be alone in a room. "Hello, hello," she called out and let her Corn Flakes go soggy, meandering through the house and entering other bedrooms, calling for me while I was in the shower. Twice. Or, she forgot where the bathroom was and yelled for my father. "Ette, where the hell are you?" The tone in her voice had changed from smooth to trembling to angry.

I reminded myself to be patient. It was Mother's Day weekend. Her presence was what I wanted.

Dressing later, my mother lifted up her tan outfit off my old maternity rocking chair. I wanted to steer her away from wearing beige so she wouldn't ask to wear her brown shoes again. She still maintained her classic style where top and bottoms matched.

"Mom, you wore that yesterday," I said and set out a pair of black pants and a button-down black sweater across the bed for her to wear.

"How do you know? Are you God, that you know what I wore yesterday?" She wagged her finger in my direction.

It was like arguing with a kid, now that I stood a few inches taller than her. "Yes, I am God and I do know what you wore yesterday." My heart fell as I bit back the words that she was the one who didn't know anything anymore.

"Well, I don't want to wear that today. I want my brown shoes." Her hands were balled into fists.

"But they don't fit," I said, quietly walking away to retrieve her thick-soled black shoes.

She followed and shouted at me from behind, "I want my brown shoes."

I envisioned a toddler having a tantrum behind my back.

With regret, I whipped open the closet door and retrieved the wedge shoes from where I had hidden them. "Here." I tossed them on the floor, exhausted, and it was only 8:30 a.m. I liked my routine and she was clearly upsetting that.

Throughout the day, my mother complained about her shoes. *They're too tight. They rub against my corns.* I dug out a shoe stretcher from the back of my closet. I had no shortage of them. I would no sooner insert and twist the wood form in the soles of her shoes, than my mother would wander off. Or misplace the stretcher after she used it. It was ironic that I could predict the path of her shoe predicament, but not that of her disease.

The routine repeated itself after a pedicure and through dinner out with our various family members.

At church on Sunday, I again felt like a tired parent with my mother in tow. I was the one with the pursed lips, telling her to be quiet as she complained about her shoes and then forgot about the shoes as she waved to the little children or leaned over and whispered, "I used to be into God and Christ."

I nodded and asked, "What about now?"

The woman who had once lined us up before church to brush off lint and ensure we wore the proper attire answered, "Not really anymore."

My shoulders finally relaxed into the hymns. Somehow my mother's disease had freed her conscience too.

After church, the sun broke through our backyard cottonwood trees and I led my mother outside. I dragged two lounge chairs around to various locations because my mother wanted to be where my father was in sight. Currently, he was nearer to the garden in conversation with Mark. My poor father couldn't get a break. I brought out my iPod and she perked up at Sinatra and finally forgot about her husband and the shoes.

"Hey, who is that?" she asked and pointed to the air as if she could see the notes of music dancing in the breeze.

I waited for her to give the answer. And finally, she did. "It's my guy." Her worry wrinkles smoothed out as she laid her head into the back of the chair.

"Summer Wind" played as I reached for her hand and swung it in the air, raising her from her chair. Welcoming spring and that easy feeling that came from the warmth of the air and the lightness that came with new growth, we swayed to the gentle wind, blowing soft kisses across the patio in tune with the music. It was the only time my mother didn't ask for her brown shoes.

Despite my mother's incontinence removing her from the Mother's Day cookout at times, she ate one-half of her lemon dessert. But when we raised our glasses and toasted to the mothers, my husband's and mine, my mother ignored the tribute, distracted by the sugary treat on someone else's plate.

"Hey, Ette, that looks good," my mother said. She forked at and gobbled down all of her husband's dessert.

I was deflated. I couldn't finish my plate. It was clear that Mother's Day didn't have any real significance for her—except that she was with those who loved and understood, if not always tolerated, her. It had only been me pushing for significance to that day on the calendar, that moment in time.

The following day, Mark and I drove my parents back to Amherst in a rental van because our car was in the shop. We made a few more stops than usual for the bathroom (Mom), the bathroom again (Mom) and gas.

I helped buckle my father into the bucket passenger seat after the final gas stop.

When I went to my mother's side, she reached for me with her long fingers and cradled my arms. "Love you."

"Love you too, Mom." I stayed there for a moment, my arm resting on hers. Chills embraced my body as I saw something like a map in her eyes that reminded me of my son. Not the color or the shape. It was like decoding one's DNA, a link to our past, a light on our future.

I had been parenting my mother as she returned to a child-like state, leading her to bathrooms, telling her what to wear or what shoes not to wear. Hiding the pair I didn't like.

I pulled the seatbelt strap down across my mother's shoulder and the belt lock clicked into place. My heart beat faster as I realized this role reversal was only going to get worse.

MOM HATES MY HAIR

In which I learn why I should change my hairstyle.

I nside a café one early afternoon, I sat across the table from my mother, with my father at her side. There was little noise and few distractions other than a buck's head hung on the wall. On weekends and during sporting events, the restaurant turned rowdy, but that day the only patrons were a businessperson slurping on beer foam and a group of elderly women playing rummy and yelling, "Yahoo!"

There would be plenty of ears to hear the conversations with my parents about long-term care and my mother's incessant rants about my hair. "It's such a mess," she said with her hands circling the air around my head.

I looked over at the older women playing cards. Why couldn't my mother have been one of them? I held back a response and scooped up the menu instead.

Years back, at another family table, an oval one because we were an uneven-numbered family, my mother had sat looking over headlines of *The Lorain Journal* newspaper, her eyeglasses with a pink-tinted frame falling down the bridge of her nose. She had yet to be diagnosed with dementia. But the care of my aging parents had been on my mind. My sister had sold them a long-term insurance policy and I wanted to get my mother's financial perspective about her prospects for a long life. "Oh, I don't get involved in those matters much," said the woman who maintained the family checkbook over the years and once chastised my father for not educating her more about the family finances. She insisted she did not have acumen for anything to do with money, despite working in a payroll department as a twenty-something-year-old.

"Well, you know, if something happens to Dad," I had said and glanced down at my bowl of a grapefruit half, which my father still cut when I visited, "I'll take you in." The joke was there were certain children she did not want to live with.

"Thanks, 'Net,'" she had said and returned to reading the newspaper.

Now, my parents were visiting Cincinnati for a few days, and our next destination was one I didn't know if they were ready for. After lunch, we were scheduled to tour a senior living community that offered a continuum of care with independent living options through dementia support, located a mile from my home. I could walk or bike there. My kids, too. Nervously, over BLT sandwiches, I talked with my father about money and selling the family home. My mother didn't seem to realize or care that selling the house meant moving, though she would have in her previous state.

I tried to steer the conversation along its natural course, but my father diverted the flow. "The best BLT I ever ate in Cincinnati was down at Findlay Market." He was referring to Paula's Café.

"They moved," I said, chewing through my bacon.

"Remember how your sister Laura planned for dinner and she would tell us, 'The place is right down the street?' And we drove to the west side from the east side just for dinner?" It was something Cincinnatians didn't often do.

He rolled his eyes in jest.

"You were a great driver, Dad. Turned us all into a family of drivers, well some with a few more wrecks to our name," I said, trying to make my father feel important, as several decisions in his life were now being driven by me. "You would drive for miles to melon, fish and corn festivals. It was nothing for you to drive to the other side of Cleveland for the Feast of the Assumption in Little Italy, if we got to eat the cannoli made by your aunt."

My mother nodded along. She opened her mouth at the word *cannoli*. "Now that sounds good," she said.

I patted my mother's hand and turned back to my father. "You know, if you moved now," I said, thinking about the buildings we were about to tour, "you would be right down the street!"

Our voices rang out in the space as the customers emptied out.

My mother's facial expression changed. Her nose crinkled.

I waited for her to say something about a move.

"Oh Annette, you're the best," she said and pointed at me. "But something you should have changed a long time ago was your hair. I don't like those strings coming out of it." She stabbed at the air again. "You have one, two, three, four. Why can't you do something about them?"

I ran my fingers along the strands of hair floating across my cheeks and pushed them behind my ears. Tears leaked out of my eyes. People stopped me on the street to ask for the name of my hair stylist.

My mother had started to cut her words sharper than the edges of her Christmas cookies. The night before, she had said to my husband, Mark, "Hey you've got a pot there," and lightly punched him in the stomach. To my sister Laura, she'd said, "Hey, you need a little sun on your legs."

As she mocked my hair, I tried to brush off her criticism by thinking about some of her positive traits. I recalled her always telling me, in a soothing voice, *It will be okay*, especially after my first husband, Devin, died. But overall, despite the disease beginning to alter her memory, it had not yet altered her character. She had always spoken her mind, just not as cruelly, and constantly.

In her state of cognitive decline, my mother also continued along the same lines of an idea for hours at a time, unless someone introduced a new subject matter. As we drove to the prospective community, road signs for Wendy's and billboards for plastic surgery relieved her of the desire to pummel me on the topic of hair.

Nervously, we entered the main door to the complex of apartments and offices like three children on the first day at a new school. The interior of the main building was lit by fake streetlamps and high skylights that allowed for sunshine to stream into every gathering space.

Our guide led us through a labyrinth of buildings and living rooms, cafeterias and nurses stations. At one point, my mother grabbed my arm. "I don't know where we are. I want to go home," she said. Her fear had steered her away from my hair.

"Just one more room to view," I assured her after we looked at a two-bedroom apartment, and peeked into the assisted living and skilled nursing areas. I patted the arm of her gray pea coat.

When we returned to my house, my mother wandered into the kitchen while my father and I sat in my burgundy-painted family room. Afternoon light flooded the couch and shone on my father's unshaven face while my dog, Enzo, licked at his hands.

I couldn't look long at the man who used to bounce me on his knees, so I dove right into the topic at hand. "If you get the two-bedroom, is that plenty of space for you?"

"Reminds me of our little house on Ridgeland Drive," he said. From the couch, he called out to my mother, "D-doesn't it, Jean? How we made do with little space?" He stumbled over his words as he looked over at my mother, who was watching the red cardinals flit about on the feeder out the window. His gaze was not reciprocated and he looked outside too.

On Ridgeland Drive, two of my sisters and I had slept in one bedroom. My brother and baby sister had slept in the other. My mother had always said, "We were happy there. Maybe because we were more together with little room to spare." It was so easy to go back in time when we didn't want to move forward.

"Did you like the kitchenette? I know it's small, but honestly neither of you are cooking. You can make soup, cereal, and have your meals in the dining room," I said, forging ahead.

"Do you think there's enough room for both couches, from the family room and living room?" my father asked, his face contorted with worry about transporting life in its entirety two-hundred-some miles.

I sensed my father's growing mental dependence on me. Whatever he was slowly letting go of was falling on my shoulders and I felt like I was bending over to receive the mantle. I retrieved a piece of graph paper from the kids' stash in the kitchen cabinet and drew out a floor plan to show where each piece might fit.

He took hold of the graph paper, his hands shaking. In the early stages of Parkinson's, he had taken medication to get the tremors under control. But now his hands trembled from something else.

My mother entered the family room and joined my father on the couch. "Hey Annette," she said, interrupting. I looked up, grateful she knew who I was.

She pointed her finger again. I could feel the heat coming off the end of her fingertips.

"You know, when I first met you," she said, "I thought to myself, she is cute and all, but she needs to change her hair."

My neck and shoulders tightened. We had met in the womb when I had no hair, I wanted to scream.

She went on. "Can't you pull it back or something and get rid of those things sticking out of your head?" She jumped up with the energy of my puppy and walked over to where I was seated on a gold, velour chair.

I sat stiff, preparing for a blow, wondering if I would hit her back. Anything to divert me from the task of unseating my parents from the family home.

"This is gonna hurt," she warned me, "but you know, get rid of these things." She yanked at the wisps of blonde that framed my face, pulling as hard as when she'd made my pigtails in first grade.

"Owww." I squeezed my eyes shut.

When I opened them, I saw my father's eyes, their whites, and not their deep coffee color. We were both stunned.

But I had gained my mother's attention. She was thinking about me. She was loving me. My mother pulling on my hair was better than my mother lost in her dementia, unable to comprehend a move from her roots.

MY MOTHER'S
CHRISTMAS GIFT

In which my mother tells me something I'd never known.

Through the twinkling lights in the artificial trees, my mother waved to me from the back row of the choir like a girl who spotted her parents while performing in her first concert.

I hadn't heard my mother's singing voice in many years, other than at funerals if we attended one together. Even then, I could always detect her voice above all others, as if she floated in a higher plane.

My parents had recently moved to their independent living apartment in Cincinnati. They were allowed to live there independently because my father's mind was intact—if not his interest in signing Christmas cards—and the two of us, with my mother still signing her name, managed to get the cards out anyhow. An outside caregiver, Elizabeth, accompanied my mother once a week to give my dad a break and was tasked, by me, to get my mother to participate in activities around the community, in particular, choir.

If my mother possessed one singular gift from above, it was her ability to sing. In her first choral performance since moving from Amherst, I would hear the voice that gripped me whenever I was in her presence and the hairs on my body stood on point.

Their center's living community published monthly calendars boasting of all sorts of field trips: Cracker Barrel and a movie, the Mighty Wurlitzer at Music Hall, Sharon Woods in Lights. Many of those my father took advantage of, but my mother's outings were limited in scope because of her attention span, incontinence and sundowning. Separated from my father—her anchor—or made anxious by the oncoming dusk, she often desired a return home before the bus pulled out from the lot.

Also within the community, a bossy piano player, Alice, directed residents who participated in choral practice once a week. The group was called The Choraliers and performed for various audiences in-house, for visiting families and also traveled to give concerts at other senior centers. They were a well-known act.

At my urging, my mother had joined The Choraliers. Elizabeth escorted her to practices. No one had any idea how long she might sit. But Elizabeth was paid by the hour, so it didn't matter to her. On one occasion, my father took her and was forced to sing along. He didn't go again. I sometimes went instead. I was also encouraged to sing. The director often curled her lip at my hoarse, off-key contribution, but she wanted my mother there for the honeyed harmony her voice offered to the group so my warbling was tolerated.

It was the first time I'd understood what it was like to live inside a senior living community and not on the outer edges as a visitor. Perhaps I should have lived there first. I sunk into a feeling of loneliness—and the need to fit in. My father, with his wits about him, didn't have the same challenges as my mother in assimilating, despite how much he complained. But I pressed my mother further into the flow of life there. I needed her to fit in.

The week before the choir's performance for their peers, my parents had come to my house after we had attended church services and eaten bagel sandwiches. It had become our Sunday ritual.

My father watched the football game in the family room. My mother and I busied ourselves in the kitchen, where the sun shone on the white Corian counter. In a stainless steel bowl, I mixed up the ground meat and other ingredients for meatballs—a recipe I am not at liberty to share—and cleared space on the counter for a measuring cup filled with water and a tray lined with wax paper. The nutty aroma of the grated Romano cheese, our favorite Italian stinky one, filled the air. Could my mother smell home?

I led my mother to her place in front of the bowl and tray, and we began to conduct our symphony of holiday traditions.

Though her mind was forgetful, my mother's hands were not. She removed her wedding ring and quickly dipped two fingers in the water, patted them on her palms, scooped up a hunk of the ground mixture and rolled and rounded the meatballs. She smoothed waxed paper across baking sheets, plopped the balls on the trays and inserted them in the freezer.

I did the same. And, side by side, we padded and balled globs of meat while Christmas songs rang out in the background.

My mother halted for a moment, staring off, then scraped at her wet and sticky fingers. "What are these for?"

Alternately rolling meatballs and watching football on TV with the Cleveland Browns on the losing end to Cincinnati, I answered, "Wedding soup." The season of Christmas was always accompanied by Italian wedding soup.

"But whose wedding?" She elbowed me and used her elbow again to point to school photos of my junior high and high school-aged kids.

"Not them. It's no one." I focused on making the meatballs as perfect as hers.

"Then why are we doing this?" She wiped her hands on an old apron with green apples that had belonged to her.

I turned my head. She wasn't angry. Instead, she blinked at me several times. I waited for the bells in the Christmas melodies playing in the background to ring a bell in her head about the season, the event, the tradition.

"What am I doing?" she asked in a soft sweet voice that dripped with a pure innocence.

"We always do this, Mom. You—always do this. It's Christmas."

Though she had been singing along to Christmas carols on a CD player and preparing to perform in a choral concert, the concept of "the most wonderful time of year" was lost. Her memory of Christmas—like her Twelve Days of Christmas ornaments—was now in storage. I dropped my last meatball and ran warm water over my hands, a comfort to my sadness. Of all the people I knew, my mother had kept Christmas closest to her heart.

I switched the music to Frank Sinatra.

"Okay," she said as she happily whiled away the rest of her rolling with his music on her lips.

I wanted to push her more into making connections with the past. But she was content with the present.

When shaping the meatballs was complete, she walked across the wood floor toward the front door and stopped mid-step. I watched as she ran her grimy hands along the khaki green walls and white woodwork. "Mom," I called out to get her to stop. In my bossiness, I didn't realize she required a guide. Her hands held fast next to the painted white column. And in two steps, she peeked out the sidelights of the door where the sun cut through. She wanted to gaze out and ground herself in the world.

Doors and windows. My mother pressed her nose and hands up against them.

My mother tried several times to unlock the deadbolt without success. The front door remained closed. She said, "You know, I always loved to sing. Ever since I was little." There was a wistfulness to her voice, as if turning away from the door she was turning ten again.

Her words bounced through the foyer.

"What?" I had heard her, but her face remained hidden by a wall.

When we were little, my mother had gathered us up like little goslings and we'd attended Midnight Mass together so she could sing in the church choir. She was also part of the Resurrection Choir that performed at all the funeral masses. Her voice, though not booming, was pitch-perfect, and she conveyed all her devotion through just a few notes of music.

She marched into the kitchen again, picked up a raw meatball and was about to eat it before I lunged across the counter and removed it from her grasp.

"I wish I would have learned how to sing when I was little," she said. Her face registered nothing, the wistfulness was gone. It was like someone had told her to say this and perhaps she didn't believe in it.

I peered into her brownish eyes that ran to light green. They brightened as she stood in a flood of afternoon light. I handed her a wet towel. "What do you mean?"

She wiped her long, slender hands on a damp paper towel. "I wanted to know how to sing." The tone in her voice deepened. She let out a long sigh. A dream unfulfilled or denied?

"Oh, like taking lessons?" I asked. "Like when you made us take piano or flute lessons or whatever everyone else played?"

"Well, yes, something like that." She mysteriously beamed and walked off, her body shifting side to side into the family room to perform her other task at my home, sliding the plantation shutters shut. She had acquired a new habit of opening and closing, opening and closing cabinets, doors and windows in my home as if she were a bi-valve, letting in only nutrients and air.

When I was ten, my mother often said, "Play my music," as she snuck into our seafoam green living room or tossed her dust rag on the floor and joined me on the piano bench to sing along. She would pop out a few notes or sing the whole song if I could play it through. And sometimes, she waved my father's old tee shirt turned rag around as if she were working a crowd.

In those moments seated at the piano, had my mother wanted to sing professionally? Is that what she meant by *something like that*? She assumed I understood the meaning, but I didn't.

 Now at the holiday performance, the choir facing the audience, my mother began to wave non-stop. Dressed in a casual, cream sweater with a blue top underneath and black slacks, she called out from her chair, "Hey, come sit here," and she motioned for me to sit next to her in the choir section. "Come here."

"I'll sit there." I signaled toward my father already seated. I didn't want to be a distraction to a woman who lately was always so distracted or aggravated if she didn't get what she wanted that instant. I feared she would direct some snippet of anger toward me or the crowd, and stand up and walk out.

The rest of the choir, men and women, older, younger, those in wheelchairs or those able to walk, proceeded in, slowly filling in the choir chairs and offering something else to hold her attention. And the musical journey down memory lane commenced.

From her roost in the rear, my mother waved me down again as if I had only now just arrived. I shrugged it off and mouthed the words as the director accompanied the singers on "O Christmas Tree" and "It Came Upon A Midnight Clear" and other well-known carols.

Suddenly, I heard her beautiful voice, soaring and lush, as she sang the opening words of "White Christmas."

I tried to join in but my words came out garbled. I sobbed as images of my mother's past Christmases floated in the air on the winds of the melodies. Her beautifully-decorated home, with a tree for every room, the school ornaments of ours she had preserved which were prominently hung on the main tree because we had more than one, and her perfectly-round meatballs. The Christmases she wouldn't remember. Ones like this that I would.

But my mother? She was the performer. Our acting chops came from her. She wasn't preoccupied with those same memories. She was focused on the present and didn't miss a note. She sang happily and joyfully through to the end.

When I was five, my mother gave me a Mrs. Beasley doll for Christmas. In high school, she bought purple corduroys for my Christmas present. Over the years, her selections were conscious choices gleaned from scribbled lists, dog-eared pages of the Sears catalog or a whisper from one of my sisters. Mrs. Beasley eventually went to live at Goodwill and the cords hunkered down in a younger sister's closet. Nothing from Christmas ever lasted, I'd once thought.

But at eighty-four years of age, though my mother didn't know, the best gift she gave to me was for keeps. It was *something like that*.

LESSONS AFTER
A BURGLARY

In which I recover what was stolen from my mother.

T en years old, with a neighbor woman at my side, I entered my family's small ranch home through the screened breezeway. The door to the house was ajar. A large gash had been chopped off the edge of the door. The neighbor pulled me back. "Someone's in there," she whispered as my siblings and I heard banging noises in the back of the house. She yanked all of us outside to the driveway and ran to call the police.

My parents arrived shortly after. They were horrified. Someone had broken into our home during the funeral of Grandpa DeLuca on my mother's side. In the rear hallway, the light revealed a broken window in the back bedroom.

"People read obituaries, then target the families," the patrolman later said.

I had also been curious about my grandfather's obituary, but for a different reason.

My mother's parents, Raffaela and Vincenzo, were married in a hilltop town in the Abruzzo region of Italy in 1920 when she was twenty-two and he was twenty-seven. My grandfather made several round trips from Italy to a small town in midwestern Ohio. In May of 1927, with Raffaela, he made one more round trip and set his sights on Astoria, New York where Raffaela's mother, Annatonia, had migrated. Raffaela arrived carrying a new life inside her womb.

That new life was my mother, Jean. But there would be a tragic end to the marriage and to the American Dream. My grandfather contracted encephalitis while working in the steelyards of Baltimore, Maryland. He died before my mother was born.

What would my grandmother do? Where would she go with a baby not yet born? She left New York with her brother, John Scurti, and landed back in Ohio, a long ways by train from New York.

A single mother, Raffaela lived with her brother next door to a family of four sisters. When the baby arrived, she was named *Vincenzella*, after her father. But the sisters pleaded, *No give an Italian name, she need American one.* They settled on *Jean*, wiping out another trace of her father. The Italian sisters, not as new to America, set about to protect a fatherless daughter from being enslaved by a stigma. They gave my mother the gift of fitting in.

Only she didn't. Her family didn't. The single mother and child relocated to Lorain, Ohio, when Raffaela remarried Grandpa DeLuca. The name in the obituary. The man I mourned, the man who smoked cherry scented pipes and smoked more cigarettes than his health could handle.

But the blood connection I had cried over was not one after all. He was of the same town, but not the same family. And for Italians, that mattered too.

Reading the obituary as a youngster, I looked for links about my mother's family that should have been printed in the paper. *Mom, can you explain your family again to me?* I asked. The story of her birth father fell from her lips once more and, by then, I was old enough to understand. *He died before I was born.* Her mantra. Her memoir. Or she cast it off. *I was an immigrant too,* having been conceived in Italy.

Back then, for my mother, the new family was an additional label that set her apart. Child of an immigrant, she had been told how to dress American, speak American, sound American. And as a stepchild, she had been told how to feel worthy of a stepfather's love.

"My stepfather wasn't always nice to me when I was younger," she said after his funeral. But in later years, that image was not the grandfather I knew. Besides, I wanted an Italian grandfather to match the other one. What did it matter if she hadn't been loved by someone who was dead? That's what was in my ten-year-old brain.

When I remarried a widower with children, my mother said again, "My stepfather didn't always treat me well." It was a warning shot to me. "Treat all of your children as if they were your own," she said to me, as a replacement for the birds and bees talk on my wedding day.

Her penchant for equal distribution of love stemmed from her own experiences. During Easter, she plopped the same number of jelly beans in all five of our Easter baskets. If we hunted plastic Easter eggs, each egg contained the same number of coins and jelly beans. The problem with that mathematical equation was she never cared who liked the yellow ones or the licorice ones best, and who didn't want the purple ones in the mix.

Rubbing up against inequality in her life, my mother strived in school, achieved National Honor Society distinction and was accepted into the a cappella choir. Separating from her life at home, where money was tight, she worked at a stove manufacturing company as a payroll clerk. Her typing skills were something I admired and I worked hard to type like her. She typed up résumés and term papers on an old Royal typewriter housed in metal casing, one dusted around in my father's office for many years. (I should have kept that typewriter from their home.)

She escaped to New York with three girlfriends and stayed at the Hotel Piccadilly for three nights and watched Dean Martin and Jerry Lewis perform in person, while sipping Liquor Galliano from a cordial cocktail glass. She was crowned a May Queen in her home parish, and crushed it on the badminton court at the Rocky Ridge Dude Ranch in the Adirondacks.

My mother was a woman of beauty and agility. And one of contradictions. She wanted us to be more like her, and yet not. She was a woman who yearned for excitement but later chastised her children, *All you kids ever want to do is have fun.*

In the mid-Fifties, the stove manufacturing plant closed. But the federal government offered teaching certificates for interested parties, and my mother grabbed the brass ring of education and earned a two-year college degree. She was the first in her family to attend college. And so, marriage waited for my mother, for her ambitious spirit to settle in, for her adventurous spirit to settle down.

She taught first grade at a small Catholic school for two years before marrying my father. Her mother, like mine, was not shy in encouraging marriage. Her mother, like mine, also had children late. She wouldn't stand for us to do so. My mother once wrote a letter to me, a year after college, where she noted, *Perhaps Anita's wedding will convince you and your sister to get serious about marriage.*

She was wrong. If I had learned anything from my mother, it was to seek life before it sought me.

About a year before I was born, my grandmother Raffaela died. I often wondered if I not only carried the family genes in terms of a larger nose and sparse, crossed eyebrows, but carried my mother's loss, her yearning for love, wisdom, and for rooting herself in an America where she and her mother had been new sprouts.

Without her mother, my mother's place in the stepfamily was tenuous, though she maintained close ties with her half-brother, Tony, his wife, Joan, and their children. Aunt Joan came from a larger Italian family and my mother envied her for that. (I suspected that's why my mother had so many children, so we didn't have the issue of envy. But we did.)

On my father's side were a scant number of relations, too. But my father's family was more prominent in the community. My mother took another step toward fitting in by marrying into a family shoe business, Januzzi's Shoes. While my mother had gone to college, and my father hadn't, she often felt his family was above her own.

When Mark and I married in 2006, we threw all our blended families, including their in-laws, into the same dining room. But back in the 1970s, my mother sometimes felt frozen out. *Uncle Tony is going to the other side of the family for Easter.* And we were often left to hold that space of her sadness and loneliness. She overcooked to overcompensate and overlooked the boisterousness of children seated before her at the table. Mostly, she would drop her fork on the plate and exhale. *Can't we just have some adult conversation?*

Regardless, her cooking was new Italian, think zucchini casseroles, while also giving a nod to the old traditions of fried polenta. She learned at the elbow of her mother, but also at the hands of her mother-in-law, Grandma Januzzi. In a blank recipe book given to my mother for her marriage, her mother-in-law wrote, *To Jean - Cooking is an art, and one of the best hobby [sic] I know.* And while Grandma Januzzi taught my mother how to turn food into art, it was Grandma Raffaela who had shown her how to give it soul.

Married, but late, and having five children, also late at that too—as my mother would bemoan—cooking never was a chore, but instead her salvation. It was her way of finally fitting in. Of being accepted.

My mother's closest friend, Mary Jane, once said, "Your mother could have been a successful caterer," and she was right. Many more compliments came over the years, originated by my mother's Italian friends.

After my Grandma Raffaela died, my mother still had a few years left with Grandma Januzzi to extend her cooking knowledge, and my mother was nothing if not the best student in the class. It was not unheard of that when I was in college, and continuing through my career, she showed up in my dorm and later at my office with lasagna, sauce, and meatballs so tender I had to eat them with a spoon in case they might crumble with a fork.

One day, I found many of my mother's mementos that helped fill in the empty spaces of her timeline. My mother was a cataloguer of life. She saved everything, but what good was it if I didn't understand the meaning behind what was saved?

Her journal from a trip she made to California? It wasn't a journal. It was a log where she noted how much money she and two friends spent, what motels they stayed at and how many miles they traveled along the way. But she never wrote an obsessive, young-woman-crush note about men she met (a few photos hinted she might have been smitten or at least curious), or how the sun rose like a yawn one day over the Pacific Ocean, the first time she had seen the ocean. There were no stories beneath her photos, or none I could remember.

She kept her life buttoned up. Smile—and leave behind the past. Smile—accept the present. Smile—move to the future. She kept so much hidden that I often wondered if the weight of those memories acted as a ballast. And while it was dementia that allowed her to float free—fury, laughter, whatever came one day to the next—it was also the disease that kept me from finally asking the questions I should have asked long ago.

It'll be okay, 'Net, my mother said, as I cried over a breakup in high school, my first. *It'll be okay,* she told me, when I was raising my son alone. *It'll be okay,* she said in later times, as part of her lexicon that dementia had not taken. That's what she told herself all those years. It was not only her devotion to Mother Mary and Jesus that caused her to think that way, but my mother possessed stores of resilience—a resilience that astounded me.

When my own disposition couldn't find its way in the dark, hers was the flashlight that said, *It'll be okay.*

The night of the break-in after my grandfather's funeral, the burglars stole my father's hunting rifles and something more precious: the wedding ring that had belonged to my grandmother Raffaela in her marriage to Vincenzo. They stole the last of what my mother had left of her family ties. And the obituary served as a reminder of how easily life could be confiscated by memory.

MOVING AGAIN

In which I learn the meaning of home.

My sister Jeanne had called me. My parents weren't happy—especially my father—in their two-bedroom, independent living arrangement. It wasn't home.

Immediately, I dialed my parents' number and went right for the punch line when my father answered. "Dad, you're not happy."

"Now, 'Net Marie, before you go and get started—" His voice shook. I imagined he held the phone away from his ear. He knew what kind of trouble I would stir up.

"—I'll move you back if that's what you want," I said to him over the phone, sounding a bit like the father he once was, threatening to turn the car around on family trips. Then I shouted it again. "I'll move you back!"

I was devastated. And mad.

Months before, we had toured every care community within a reasonable distance from the family home in northern Ohio. The three of us, my father, mother and me, toured senior living centers that resembled museums with thick marble columns and those with all the liveliness of a graveyard. My father was like Goldilocks at every turn, unable to find one that fit just right. It was an impossible task, trying to find a place that worked for him because he could live with little support, and for her because she couldn't.

When my parents, again, mainly my father, settled on living near me in Cincinnati in a community with services ranging from *hands-off* to *someone please keep track of me*, I thought that decision was for the best. Mostly by default, I was their designated power of attorney, the executor, and all around get-it-done person. I both feared and wanted this job so I showed up because I couldn't imagine not showing up. That was my approach to life. I needed to overcome that which scared me; it was an adrenaline rush of sorts.

My parents' new apartment was located on my route to eat, work, play, then home. Some nights, I glanced up at their third floor apartment and could see lights glowing in the same way my father had left the lights on for us as teens when we stumbled in near dawn. I crossed my fingers that their move had been the right decision.

In his former home, my father once lost his balance, dropped to the linoleum floor, and hit his head. Despite the proximity of my sister Jeanne, he called no one while his wife with dementia helped wipe up his blood. But now there was oversight to keep those instances from happening again.

Over the phone, my father relented. "I can do this, but it isn't easy with your mother, you know."

Of course, I knew. That explained the difficulty we had in locating a comfortable setting for them.

"But if you keep helping us, that's good." His tone evened out until he complained again about the staff not cleaning his sweaters properly, my mother's bathing habits, the lack of options in ice creams flavors at dinnertime.

My father needed an outlet for his anger about my mother's memory problems more than he needed a move back home.

"It's gonna be fine, 'Net Marie," he assured me. And I had to trust him and tell him the same. We only had each other by then.

Then the progression of his Parkinson's caused more shaking, weakening his muscles. During one tumble, my father's elbow scraped against the sharp edge of the kitchen table and he incurred a large gash. Every morning for a week, I drove him to the local hospital's wound care center. I walked through the corridors with my relentlessly curious and incontinent mother locked onto one arm, and my father clasping at my other arm while I carried a backpack overflowing with my mother's Depend underwear and snacks. He was assigned a walker, but refused to use it at the hospital, and given the coarse carpeting in their apartment, could barely shove the thing across the floor. I watched how difficult it was for him and ached inside but said nothing. I started to feel helpless too.

Phone calls from the staff at their living community arrived twice daily. My mother could still walk at warp speed and, without detection, she had wandered out the door into the circular driveway where life squads and buses pulled in regularly.

My father called repeatedly, mostly about the television, mainly to talk. "Yeah, that remote control for the TV and cable Mark bought isn't working again."

The amenities at the center were plentiful but reality was not one of them.

One morning, I signed my father up for a breakfast outing at Perkins while I joined my mother in a smaller dining room where the staff thought she might be more comfortable. She didn't have much to say, so we read the *Cincinnati Enquirer*. I urged her to read, believing that might save some part of her mind, the part that once read *Where the Wild Things Are* or Dr. Seuss to me. Neither my mother's prodigious reading skills nor her handwriting had diminished. Yet, she never wrote much of anything anymore, her pen unable to follow her wriggling thoughts across the page.

My father returned from his outing, weary. His cheeks were drawn in and their former chunkiness drooped toward his jawline. He was tired— tired from the erratic ways in which my mother's disposition altered. She was belligerent, skeptical, not recognizing me at times. She set herself apart in crowds at choir or lunch, and said little. I would have been angry, too, if I knew I was losing my memory and, slowly, my husband.

I often bathed my mother, as she was distrustful of revealing herself to the staff. "Mom, it's warm, I promise," I said and led her near the bath water. She pulled at my arm and in doing so, my rotator cuff tore. The pain lasted for days. I planned for surgery—when I had time.

The more belligerent my mother became, the more my father's mental and physical capabilities declined. He struggled with remembering to take new medications, and his current ones. In the middle of the night, he called me. "That damn cleaning crew stole my wallet," he said, breathing heavily.

"Dad, are you sure? That's just not likely." He had torn the apartment upside-down looking for it.

In the morning, as I joined him in the search, we discovered it—in his hiding place.

There came a morning when my father, groggy, not knowing his surroundings, didn't rise from bed. The delivered breakfast trays sat unopened. According to the director, the food had not been touched by him or my mother. Rushing to their apartment, I found my mother dutifully sleeping at her husband's side. His speech slurred and his mind was in a haze. He required the attention of a doctor and was admitted to the hospital.

My visiting siblings and I tended to my father while trying to unravel the mysterious events that led to his hospitalization. The first night without my father, my mother spent in my home, wandering aimlessly through the night. In the morning, I realized I needed more help than a village. In haste, I was forced to move my mother to the care center's dementia unit.

My father's vital signs were weak, but within range. His CAT scan and MRI were clear. The doctors were perplexed. They released him to the rehabilitation center.

My mother's temporary unit and the rehab center were across the parking lot from their apartment. She was staying down a short hallway that connected to the rehab center. My father, if he improved, could visit. His progress came first in baby steps, then stopped and reeled backward. Soon, he was lying prone in a hospital bed—again.

And I was left with my mother. She was ripping at window shades in the dementia unit. Despite her proximity to my father, it wasn't where I wanted her to be long-term. It was a unit, single and complete, yet not really a home. A home contained a separate room for eating and watching TV. In a home, I was free to walk in and out of the doors. In a home, I could visit with a key and not have to sign a log and press a button to visit my mother. In a home, my mother would still look stylish. I could help her achieve perfection. I knew little about what a monumental task it might be to find a home for someone with dementia.

Depressed and debilitated, my father lay in his hospital bed down the street from my mother. But I could not let the location of my mother's unit in relation to my father determine what was best for her.

No matter what, my parents couldn't return to their apartment. My father would require a little more oversight, and should my mother need to move full-time into a dementia unit, she could not go on living permanently in that small unit. I wouldn't let her.

Pushing forward once more, I visited any and all surrounding care communities where the two of them could be joined together again. I was certain that would happen. One center was near my son's high school, which he would attend for two more years. He could participate in service outings to visit his grandmother, and it was near the writing center where I taught.

Look for the light, I thought, as I toured the place near the high school, because that's what I would want. Popcorn machines and potted palm trees added color to an already sunny interior, despite clouds forming outside. The smell of sugar filled the room as an aide set out freshly baked oatmeal cookies. The residents' hairstyles were lovely, not a hair out of place. Their clothes matched and were not rumpled. A white fence circled the back yard. In the faces of the nurses and caregivers, I saw pools of compassion.

Assuming everything, including my father, would be okay, I decided to move my mother there to one of the secure living areas. She would attend a salon appointment weekly, the priest from the local Catholic church across the street would arrive for Communion, and movies from "her day" would be shown on a large screen in a room with surround sound. *Check, check, check.*

A week after my mother's move, without my father and in a strange new setting, my mother struck out with the full force of the separation from her husband. Anyone who was in her way heard her bellow, *Get the hell away from me.*

One day, the nurse called. "Your mother hit one of the residents— Jane." This time it was my mother setting in motion the beginning of another chapter in a book I didn't have time to read.

"Clobbering is a substitute for her confusion," I pleaded with the care director. Didn't the caregivers understand non-verbal communication? Phone calls continued. Her hitting extended to the staff. I was informed she needed medication. "A last resort," the nurse told me. A last resort when this was her first month at the home?

My mother was not violent, unless I considered her brandishing of a wooden spoon when we lied or talked back as kids. She was a happy person. She exuded warmth. She was loved by so many of her friends, friends who would write, *I miss your lovely face—and your cooking*, friends I had separated her from, and were added to a list of separations for her—a continent, a father, a firstborn, a husband, a home, a mind…a friend.

And now, the doctor prescribed anti-psychotic medication for a woman my siblings and I had once tormented and accused of being psychotic when she had thrown our shoes—which were not put away in the cardboard carton in the garage—out into the drifts of Ohio snow. Only we had been joking, whereas the staff at her new home saw her as someone who experienced a series of psychotic episodes, and not as a mother, a woman in pain. She would have to move if I didn't allow for her to be medicated. Move? Were they kidding? I couldn't allow that to happen one more time. They also wanted a paid caregiver to watch over my mother—when the center was already being paid to care for her.

Then, my father died. His cause of death was listed as "complications related to Parkinson's," but I believe he died from the loss of his co-pilot in life.

My mother had been the navigator on our family road trips, circling attractions on the TripTik, calling out stops for food and hotels. With his left hand on the wheel, my father's arm rested on the open window frame, while his gold watch gleamed in the sun. With his right hand, he would slip a Necco Wafer in his mouth to keep from yelling at the kids in the back seat. That had been our life.

But my father had reached a point where he no longer had my mother at his side. No one to direct him to the gas station, or to tell him he'd taken the wrong exit. No one to tell him he had bought the wrong color of geraniums for the front landscape beds or that he hadn't hung the Christmas lights in a straight line. No one to say, *It'll be okay.*

The drugs prescribed to my mother wore off, but the feeling that I had failed did not.

My father had owned a large stamp collection and was reluctant to part with it because of its perceived value. In the end, selling the stamps didn't add much to the bottom line of his finances. But his leaving my mother with me was a different treasured possession. I might know what was best for her, but my caregiver knowledge was years old and related to my first husband's cancer and not an aging population, though one student in my writing circle had said, "You're really good with old people."

Yet I had struggled with the old people in front of me. Perhaps because I never saw my parents as old as they were. My parents were born in the same month of the same year, and my mother had birthed children late in life. Ashamed of her age, she often hid her driver's license from me. I didn't know her real age until I was fourteen or so.

I needed to move my mother before they put her out of the front door but when I asked friends and colleagues about living communities for people experiencing dementia, many said, "We're not there with my parents, yet," and added, "thank God."

A neighbor's mother had resided at another memory care community, again near my son's high school, my work, and en route from the suburbs into the city. I hesitated. Convenience was not going to be a factor this time.

I steered up the short driveway of Arden Courts where a flag waved in the wind and read, *Memory Care*. Without my father, my mother—the overachiever—had skipped over assisted living and any sort of skilled nursing care, and proceeded to the front of the line. Crossing the threshold of another white-fenced porch, I sensed a theme in the exterior of the places I visited. Bright and happy. Little did any executive know if my mother found so much as a chip on that white paint, not only would the maintenance man hear about it, we all would.

On a tour with the young marketing director, I passed through the second secure door. Windows on either side of the hallways circled and met up with a light-filled community room in the rear. Hallways ran off the four corners and down those corridors, where residents were separated into groups of fifteen, each group with its own kitchenette, family room, shower and tub rooms, laundry, and a door to the outside. Each group had its own home-like setting.

"She can be outside most of the day with staff checks every fifteen minutes, if the weather is appropriate," the staff member said.

I wanted to move my mother in that instant, but she had to be accepted. I knew what was in her file about the hitting, but didn't want to think about it. *Another obstacle in a long line of obstacles*, my mother might have said about being the daughter of an immigrant, a daughter theoretically born out of wedlock, then a stepdaughter and, now an outlier with dementia.

From the moment my mother moved into her new setting, the trauma of her loss began to subside. Outside in the sweltering August heat, she and I pretended we were sunbathing on a Florida beach. She smiled as I read aloud poetry books to her and extended her warmth to a resident's dog even though she had never liked dogs unless they belonged to one of her children. She eased into her new chair at the kitchen table, the wooden bench in the courtyard, and the green padded conference room chairs in the activity center. And she sank into the cushions of a white wicker settee or its matching chair, propped her elbow on the chair's arm, lay her cheek in her hand and fell asleep with her face turned toward the rivulets of the sun's rays.

Her hitting had been my mother's way of ordering me *I need to move on*. I overheard stories about loved ones whose family moved a mom or dad from one care setting to another, only to have the parent die soon after. Often the family blamed the new circumstances on the staff, but I saw the change in scenery as a chance for my mother to settle into her soul. If she was at peace, she could go on with her life, or could let go of it without guilt. Something my father couldn't have done.

My father had given up his flourishing garden and our family's steady supply of Roma tomatoes, but his ultimate sacrifice had been to move for my mother. I knew it before he stopped tilling the ground in the spring, before he left Amherst, and on the day he died. And I knew it when I eventually moved my mother into a home specifically for memory care. I just hadn't been able to do anything about it while my father was alive. His living conditions and the family finances had been dependent on where my mother could be safe, if not thrive. Their apartment had been comfortable for them, but nothing that followed would have been suitable—for him.

I hadn't really understood my mother's dementia, and, over the past nine months, my attention had been tied up in the upheaval of my parents from their hometown and the death of my father.

While my mother snuggled up with a blanket on an armchair in the TV room at Arden Courts, she asked questions repeatedly. "What are you doing here?" "Where is this?" "Where are we going?"

In her new setting, I could honestly answer, "I'm here because this is your home. We don't have to go anywhere anymore."

In which my mother finds the sun again.

"Where's Mom?" I invariably asked as a teen, whenever I wanted to stay out past curfew, borrow my mother's Chevy Caprice or be driven to a sleepover. Whichever sibling was home said, "Out there," and tilted his or her head toward the front mudroom porch.

Other times, my father would mutter, "Where's your mother?" as he wandered inside from the garden, wiping his grimy hands on his canvas pants. "Out there," I responded with powdered sugar ringing my mouth after eating one of my mother's famed nut horn cookies, craning my head toward the concrete patio out back.

My most vivid memories of my mother were of searching for her, stumbling upon her outside wrapped in the warmth of the sun. She used to threaten that she would up and leave us if we didn't put our shoes away or dust our rooms to her satisfaction, so when she was outside, it was easy to envision that she had gone missing. But no, she was just out there.

Summer days in our hometown, my mother shooed us five kids out of our 1950s brick and white vinyl-sided, 1500 square foot home on Ridgeland Drive under threat of having to vacuum or sponge down the bathtub with Scrubbing Bubbles if we stayed inside. We rode our bikes or walked across the bustling four-lane Route 58 to the public swimming pool. If one kid hung back at home or dallied over a salami and American cheese sandwich and Twinkie, she demanded to know why. She wasn't worried if that kid was sick or had fought with a friend.

She wanted us out so she could get *out there* too.

My mother had little interest in sunning at the public pool. *That's for you young kids*, she said. She saved her teal blue one-piece bathing suit with skirt-to-cover-her-slim-thighs for vacation only. I once thought her attitude was derived from modesty. But her approach had everything to do with kicking us out of Ridgeland Drive. She wanted time to herself and would drag out a vinyl folding chair and, wearing shorts, dangle her feet, white— as opposed to tan like her legs—in the plastic kiddie pool which sloped in the backyard and created a deep end for grass floaters, dead flies and her long toes.

Our family grew up. The kids put meat on their bones from eating my mother's fleshy ravioli and we moved to a home double in size of the ranch home. On Lincoln Street, my mother had plenty more room to roam, but still she chased us off and gravitated outside when the weather warmed. And even when it didn't.

When we moved, my parents bought a new set of vinyl-strapped folding chairs. In her sleeveless, boxy blouse that hid her stomach, pushed out by six pregnancies, my mother dragged one of those chairs across the concrete and shifted it from the front porch to the back patio like a sundial's shadow responds to the rays. *Getting some sun on my arms*, she would say as if she needed an excuse to sit down. Her arms fell onto the arms of the chair. Her hands drooped and her blood ran downward into her hands. The chair was someone to hold her when her legs and mind tired.

When the fiery orb pushed up the morning in the front of the house, my mother parked in a chair on the mudroom porch out front and turned her face up at the flash of sun, but not before she scolded my father for planting the salmon-colored geraniums too close together. Or clucked at a shred of mulch or white rock cluttering the sidewalk that my father hadn't swept off.

As the sun faded to afternoon, still in sandals, my mother trailed the path of its beams and carted the chair to the back of the house where the truckers drove by the highway and honked and waved. She didn't wear a bathing suit, just her everyday clothes. Truckers beeped nonetheless.

Thirty-five years later, when my parents moved to Cincinnati, they chose a two-bedroom unit ready for occupancy in the community within walking distance to me. But the only one available was on the third floor, with a balcony overlooking a wooded area that padded the view from a busy state road. We all breathed at the sight of the sun poking through branches, even if in splinters.

That first afternoon I'd viewed their apartment and deck, I had broken the quiet that had been accompanying us throughout the process. "How perfect." The sun would slice right through a stand of trees onto the narrow deck and into an open living space. There would be plenty of room for most of their furniture, other than the dining room suite, which was only used perhaps one-hundred times over the years. Looking downward, my father kept to himself, bearing the burden of decisions I had not been privy to. But my mother's hazel eyes lit up. "This is lovely."

When it came time for their move, we transported a subset of the plastic chairs in the back of the moving truck and situated them on that deck. "How perfect," my mother said. *How perfect*, I convinced myself.

Once settled, I tried to persuade my mother to join me on the balcony. She. Did. Not. Would. Not. Budge. I leaned back in through the sliding glass door and glanced quickly at my father, begging for an explanation.

"She's afraid of heights," my father said, as if reciting an encyclopedic fact.

"What are you saying?" I choked up as I watched my mother eat off a plate of leftovers from lunch.

He was wrong. She never rode roller coasters, but we hiked paths along Mt. Hood and parts of Mt. St. Helens. We stood on the precipice of many cliffs overlooking waterfalls in Oregon. "For how long has she been like this? Why didn't I know?" Before or after the dementia had cozied up alongside her life? I was disheartened. There was so much about her I didn't know, and here, my mother was already becoming a *she*, a person talked about, a person whose voice was once unwavering.

The new living space kept my mother prisoner from fresh air and independence. To get *out there* she had to use the elevator, press the correct button and carry her own chair. She would also have to remember how to get back in. She would never get *out there* I reasoned—unless by accident. How had I let that happen?

At the time of my father's death, I had been forced to undertake a second move for my mother and then another. I kept searching for a place where she could get *out there* and connect to some joy in her heart and feel the sun tickling her legs.

Now at Arden Courts, she felt the warmth emanating through the windowpanes streaked with southern Ohio pollen, and relentlessly pushed on the arm of the secure doors at her new home.

She pushed. I pushed. The fragrant out of doors, the colors *out there* beckoned her to play. Finally, she and her mind could wander free.

We walked in the autumn sun where mums poked their heads through the mulch my mother complained about. *It's messy.* Leaves from magnolia trees that fluttered across the sidewalk were *in my way*.

Dressed in a knee-length sweater, she broke free of my grasp. She dragged a wooden patio chair like an expert company mover and positioned it in the orbit of her personal solar system. The sun showered her again with a sprinkling of light, as if bathing a weary friend.

Her face glowed. She was content. I was too.

It had taken four tries, but finally my mother had found the sun again. She was *out there*.

Finally, We Find
the Right Place

In which I learn a pillow can't replace my father.

"A body pillow, what's that?" I asked Rachel, the young nurse in my mother's new care home, a home where she and I could finally relax.

"It's just a long pillow, runs the length of the body." She splayed out her long, tan arms as she surveyed my mother's form, now napping in her spartanly made bed.

"I already have two pillows for her. One is rolled up into a tube with a rubber band so she can protect her hair." My mother carted that pillow everywhere, including on planes and in cars. "The other pillow is for her legs, when she sometimes has hip pain."

There was little room left on her twin bed.

The bed. The making of it was an important task for my mother, signifying a tidy life. "She probably won't want anything more on her bed." I cast off the suggestion. The bed had been made with soft, clean sheets and a cream, lightweight bedspread. Ours had been a family that did not use duvets or comforters or toss more pillows than heads.

The nurse nodded. "I understand. But the long one can replace your dad." Her green eyes sparkled with tears.

My father. I had yet to let myself cry over his death. I was still in work mode and my purse was filled with the purple file folder that once contained a myriad of papers spelling out the directions for my parents' lives, only both had taken unexpected turns, and now the folder's contents had been reduced by half. I wasn't ready to think of my mother without my father. I still saw an image of her visiting my father in the hospital, eating his ice cream, something he no longer craved.

"She wouldn't like all that clutter," I told Rachel, then remembered, if I was going to be my mother's best advocate, I had to break myself from using *she*.

"Okay," Rachel said, but I could tell she wasn't convinced.

"It'll be harder for Mom to make her own bed," I said, though she had already stopped doing so.

My mother was an expert bed maker. She found solace in the chore.

In the afternoons when we returned from school as youngsters, I found her upstairs making one bed or the other. Certainly she heard us banging the doors, our books clunking down on the counter and the cookie drawer sliding open and shut, but always she talked to herself, asking questions like, "What should I make for dinner?" I often imagined some voice from above answering, "Meatballs."

As I grew, on Saturday mornings, my mother placed sets of sheets on my dresser. Though my father had been a sergeant in the army, it was my mother who had taught me to cut in the corners, snap the flat sheets to the top of the bed and fold over the blankets. She showed me how to fluff the pillow: shake it on the long-edge and fold back the extra flap of fabric like doing a tummy tuck on a pillow. I watched as she ran her hands to smooth out the nylon bedspread bought from a Kmart store. A ritual I continued. And she demanded I clean out what was underneath the bed. Dirty tube socks, *Anne of Green Gables*, old spirit wear, a balled up pair of JC Penney's jeans with a rip in them that I didn't want her to know about.

Making beds was always a metaphor for my mother's life. It was a metaphor in my life too. If I left the bed a mess, my life was in the same state. But for my mother, the chore entailed perfecting the folds and exemplified the feelings of hospitality, comfort and home that she extended to all who slept under her roof.

However, adding a new body pillow now to her repertoire of bedspread and rolled pillow might confuse her. The question remained, would she want the thing on her bed or not?

I begrudgingly went to HomeGoods and bought the pillow with a rough feel to its beige pillowcase. I couldn't find a satin or fuzzy one—one that she might run her hands along and *ooh* and *ahh* over its softness—and briefly considered a pillow that was full body length and shaped like a furry brown bear. However, I didn't want to scare her. She had enough to fear.

I carried the long pillow in my mother's room and placed it on her bed, nestled next to the wall. I thought back to my parents' last morning in Amherst. As the bleary sun had risen, I had run back up the steps to retrieve a book and noticed the door to their master bedroom cracked open. In bed, my mother lay facing the window and my father had his arms folded around her. The rumble of the morning train of our youth blew through their dreams. I didn't want the train's lonely whistle to wake them. I wanted to paint that image of my parents locked in an embrace, before life pulled them apart.

I wasn't at her care home in the evenings when my mother went to bed, but it wasn't long after that I discovered the pillow standing on end in the corner of her already-cramped room, banished from the bed, punished for the crime of trying to replace my father.

Her voice rang in my ear as I recalled my father's wake. In the middle of the prayer service, she had asked, "Who is in the coffin?" When I answered, "Ette," steering clear of a generic Dad, she said, "Ette," as if she were calling him inside for dinner. A pillow wouldn't have responded to my mother's call of *Ette*.

That night of my father's vigil, my mother and I had slept side by side at a motel while Mark slept in a room next to ours. It was a long night, and my mother was up several times for a drink of water, asking "Where are we?" and requiring a change of her underwear. I was grateful when the alarm finally went off, so we could carry on like normal people—washing, bathing, dressing, dispensing her medication.

Upon our arrival at church for the service, she had asked again about whose funeral we were attending. I no longer had the heart or the patience to answer. I couldn't tell her it was her beloved because I couldn't imagine her living without him. Worse, I couldn't imagine her living without memories of him.

Though the nurse at her new home wanted her to live with a pillow, someone decided, perhaps my mother, or a caregiver, that if my mother were going to do without my father, she would do without a pillow too.

But something—or someone—had to replace him.

In the past, I had lobbied for this duty without fully understanding what lay ahead. I didn't know if I could do it.

My mother wasn't always capable of understanding everything I told her. She became easily agitated. *That person is fat...What the hell do you want?* She moved toward a place of anger and anxiety. I thought she might get better. Drug companies flooded the market with medications designed to hold onto the last gasp of a memory before it died forever.

I thought I might get better. Maybe become the respectful, tolerant daughter I mistakenly thought I had been in the past.

As a young adult, I had done as I'd pleased, made my way across the country, figured out which career to pursue, or quit a job altogether without her feedback or consideration. *What did she know?* I asked back then, as I fought with her to find my own edges. And carelessly I tossed off her responses. But like any sturdy Italian, my mother trailed me determinedly at every bend. I let her walk in my shadow—never beside me.

Now, I wanted to ask my mother if my chicken cacciatore had been spiced with the necessary pinch of cayenne pepper, or tell her about one of my children who was struggling. Essentially, I wanted to ask anything and tell her everything she meant to me before she disappeared. And I wanted her to do the same.

One morning, I discovered my mother had fallen asleep on top of her bedspread. Uncertain of what mood I might find her in, I had been anxious before my visit. Tired, I lay down in her twin bed and curled my body around hers. My head rested above hers on a separate pillow, as she now had two, neither of them rolled anymore.

She woke up, turned over and caressed my face. "Ette?" she asked like a child searching for comfort after a storm.

Her question surprised me. More so, the use of my father's name. She hadn't said his name in several months. It saddened me to hear her ask for him in such an innocent manner. I didn't know if she was asking of my father's whereabouts, or if she had been hoping I was my father. I didn't know how to answer.

"Mom, he's not here," I said and brushed her tangled hair.

"Oh, dear." She rolled back over.

"He'll be around sometime," I said and rubbed her back. The words didn't come for me to say he was dead. Often, I had yet to accept it myself.

"Okay." She closed her puffy eyes once more and wiggled her back into my stomach.

Her head landed against my heart—and there I let it rest.

A DIFFERENT KIND
OF PARADE

In which my mother and I learn not to let the parade pass us by.

Like a swallow returning to Capistrano, my mother gravitated to the white wicker loveseat in her care home, her movement based on the clock and the seasons. Following lunch of breaded fish and creamy potatoes, she sat in the warmth emanating from a nearby window. And though cold that day, a brilliance had broken through the feathery yellow sky. Light bounced off the white painted chair and gave the illusion of heat.

"Lots of traffic today," I said, seated beside my mother, watching the residents move here and there along the corridors like busy ants. "It reminds me of Italy." I poked her in the ribs to keep her awake. I always talked about Italy, a place where I came to know more of my mother's heritage and through that, more of her.

My mother had been seventy-seven when she'd finally visited her parents' home country. It had been the wish of my dying husband who wanted our family to travel there together. He had understood my mother in a way the rest of us did not, perhaps because of his imminent death.

The parade of residents at the care home continued walking past the white wicker furniture as the two of us sat and chatted. I remembered watching the Italians as they walked along the streets of Rome in their tradition of *passegiatta*—a leisurely stroll—where folks came out of their dwellings in the evenings and promenaded around the piazza. Mothers sought out activities for children to get them out from under foot. Older gentlemen remained deeply engaged in the day's events while seated on crumbling, ancient walls. Young men strutted about, looking to impress the young girls, and the young girls pretended not to care.

In Rome, during our family's trip, we had sat, four daughters flanking our mother with the Trevi Fountain behind us, and observed the young men with a hunger in their eyes file past us on their way to meet girls. Tired butchers closed up shop and staggered home as the rose seller pestered beautiful young women, like my older sister, who had finally accepted a flower but gave no payment. My mother loved all the people. "They're all so beautiful," she'd said to me, her neck craned, watching the young Italian women, and perhaps the men, as we walked through Roman ruins. Her feet fell softly on time-worn dirt as if welcomed by the centuries. She was intrigued by the people and the smells, imagining her life transported to ancient times. At her age, the history was of no consequence other than the Pope and the Church. "*D'accordo, Mamma.* Everything here is *così bello*," I'd said and leaned back on a stone wall to soak in the slanting, late afternoon sun. She had done the same.

The residents continued to file by on their way to reading hour. "That was such a great trip, wasn't it Mom?" I asked, tugging at her sleeve. I wanted to know if the trip had awakened a piece she'd buried decades ago, when her parents had died. Had she sensed them walking among us? Was she walking closer to them now?

My mother nodded her head while she scrutinized every resident who marched by as if I were announcing each entry in a parade. I waited for her to lash out at someone—for she could find fault in me or the residents at any given time—about a shoe, a grin or a whisper she couldn't hear. But she was unusually quiet, as if each person who passed was a study in miracles.

A skinny resident named Peyton, wearing sturdy shoes, walked non-stop. She was on her third lap when she bumped into one of the marketing staff accompanying a new female resident and the woman's two grown sons.

"This is home," the husky, gray-bearded son said to his mom, sweeping his arms down the hallway pretending he and his mother had always lived here. The son's mother crept farther into the hallway and the other son, wearing a suit, magically appeared to escort his mother toward her new room. I listened to the exchange for a while, the lexicon and the deception all too familiar. How easily I had deceived my mother, or how, medicated by the staff of her previous care home, drugged and unaware my mother had been.

Peyton stopped and looked at me with a wrinkled brow that matched her sunken cheeks. With her military haircut, she exuded toughness. "Great, like we need another person living here." I chuckled.

Just as Peyton dropped her line, Jimbo, a male resident, paced out his laps past us. My mother shied away from Jimbo, often shooing him away. His blank stares scared her. I gazed into Jimbo's leaky eyes where I saw the fright he felt, unable to speak for himself. My eyes would have looked the same in that situation.

Jimbo circled back around, now locked arm in arm with another resident, Roger, and the two stopped while I played Frank Sinatra tunes on my iPhone, transported to a time when life made sense, or at least the music did.

The strains of "New York, New York" kicked up in volume. Another woman, Shari, with white, wild and curly hair, stopped to ask about the location of Room 43. "I honestly don't know," I said. For as much time as I spent there, I didn't know my own mother's room number yet. Maybe 13?

It really felt like a parade now as Shari rounded again, halted and waited at my side. She was also tuned in to the music. She began strutting like a proud majorette.

Agitated by the interruptions, my mother grabbed my arm. "Now wait a minute, wait a minute, wait a minute. What's that sound?" She kept poking at me in the arm.

She didn't mean *what*. She knew it was the sound of her youth before her disease, before her kids, before my father was *Ette* to her. But she couldn't always put her finger on the *who*.

I brushed the back of my hand across her cheek. "Mom, it's Frank."

"Oh, that's right," she said, laying a finger aside her nose like Santa rising up the chimney.

"Old Blue Eyes?" I asked, knowing she knew.

She gave me a stern look. "Of course it's Old Blue Eyes. Did you think I didn't know that?"

Shari stood over us, confused and still seeking Room 43. When the music hit a crescendo, her dull-green eyes brightened to emerald.

I patted the seat cushion, inviting Shari to sit. "Did you like Frank Sinatra, when you were younger?" I thought she wanted company.

"Oh yes," she clapped and remained standing.

"Did you ever see him in person?" I asked, my heart pounding. If she had, perhaps my mother had.

"Oh, once or twice, in Chicago and Indianapolis."

"Oh," I said. I looked at my mother. She said nothing. Unable to recall any past conversations about seeing her idol, I guessed I would never know if my mother had come that close to Sinatra or not.

Shari patted her left leg to the rhythms of the music. "He was a big part of my life when I was young, but I don't remember anymore." She sighed. "My mouth never shuts up, but my mind does nothing," she said and wandered away.

She really hadn't given herself credit.

There was an art to the residents' strolling. Their constant movement at a brisk or measured pace, the number of laps. All combined to represent who they were, who they remembered they were, who they still wanted to be.

My mother suddenly stood up and hurriedly walked away. She peeked around one corner, then the next, like a spy on a mission. In her sights was a poster that spelled out the commandments of health care practiced by the center. She was drawn to a blue ink blob at the bottom of the poster, fascinated by its odd shape.

She traced the line with her finger as if tracing her family history. "What is this?" she turned to ask.

Catching up, I hunched up my shoulders perplexed. She imitated my shrug and traced her finger around the blob again.

We would be staring at the blob all day, if I let her. I nudged her away from the only thing in that hallway anchoring her to the present. The only thing in the hallway that didn't make sense to me but intrigued her deeply.

We rejoined the walkers making their rounds.

My mother and the other residents, through ceaseless wandering, questioning and eavesdropping, practiced their own form of the *passegiatta*—the parade. It was how they survived the countless days that didn't add up by demonstrating to others *I am still here*. On we walked.

In which my mother makes a joke.

"There you are, 'Net!" My mother opened one puffy, red eye, watering from the aftereffects of a cold. She was slouched on a floral sofa, one arm drooping over a footstool turned armrest on her lap. The bottom of her pants rose up over her sock line to show off calves dented by the socks' elastic bands.

My heart beat faster. It had been some time since she had used my nickname. When I had called from Oregon or Cincinnati or wherever I was in the universe, my mother answered the home phone, "Oh, 'Net, I knew it was you." Before her dementia, she was convinced we were on the same wavelength, though I had gone to great wavelengths to convince myself we were not.

In my mother's world, separated now from my father, I was still "Net," but was I 'Net, the loving, sensible daughter or the pesky, parental one? And since I could no longer detect what she thought, did she still believe we existed on the same wavelength?

She sat straight up, both eyes now drawn to my running shoes. They were neon blue—think North Carolina blue—with an orange swoosh. *Uh oh*, I thought, *here it comes*.

"Hey, what are you doing with those blue shoes?" Her finger wagged at me like a dog's tail. She kicked at my shoes with her sport-cushioned ones. I was reminded of my last visit when my mother had pointed at my footwear and asked, "What the hell are those things on your feet?" When I had answered, "Rain boots," she'd instructed me to take them off. I told her, "They're my shoes for the day," and she said, "I don't care," and kicked at my boots until I removed them.

When I was little, she had taught me that pointing was rude. In her home now, no one minded his or her manners, and I loved the brashness of that. Pointing in public for the residents, for my mother, was one of the few actions that were as natural as eating.

My mother pointed toward my feet again. In the TV room where most residents were gathered, I considered breaking into an Elvis song about blue shoes, but a resident named Iris, hacking from a cough and pulling out her tucked shirt to wipe off saliva, and Dolores, another resident, staring off into space while biting her nails, probably did not want to hear me sing with my flat, hoarse voice.

Instead, I lifted up one foot and rolled it around to show off the peacock-colored footwear. "They're my running shoes, Mom. I was a runner, ran track, jumping over hurdles." I wanted to ask if she remembered telling me how track would make my thighs thicker, but I held back on that topic. "Remember all those times I fell?" I balled up my hands and made the running girl motions first then hurdling motions, right leg as lead, left leg trailing.

My junior high track career had been less than stellar, despite the fact I'd almost never lost a race. At a meet ten miles away, I'd fallen during a race and my coach had called an ambulance—and my mother. Embarrassed, I was transported to the local hospital and diagnosed with a contusion. When my mother arrived, she took in a long, deep breath, unsurprised by the kid who was always getting banged up. The woman who had bandaged all my knees let me lean on her and I limped to the car. When I got home, I boasted to my siblings and eighth-grade classmates about my contusion to cover for my embarrassment. I thought I sounded brave—but soon, I learned a contusion was simply another word for a *bruise*.

"And what about when I fell up the steps all the time, Mom? And you just curled up your lips and said, *Only you, 'Net*." I was athletic but never graceful, such that my name, when translated, meant *little grace* and I was certainly in short supply of it.

A smile crossed her face. I sensed she related to a time when she had wrapped my sprained ankles in Ace bandages and applied Neosporin to gashes in my knees and said, *It'll be okay*.

"C'mon let's get up and go walk around."

I blew on my hands to warm them up and held one out for her. She sighed, her trademark for *Quit telling me what to do, but I will probably listen to you anyhow,* and took hold, inching to the edge of the couch. The footstool rolled off her knees and onto the carpet, and she pushed herself up.

We wandered from her hallway into the main gathering space and encountered two male residents, Terry and Richard, actively engaged in a conversation

Terry, the engineer, said, "Well, if you at run this, does not you tell look back."

Richard, the airman, mumbled his reply. "Should people leave how to work airplanes, they ride them make."

My mother smirked and threw up her hands. *Word salad,* as the staff sometimes called those exchanges, followed some grammatical sentence structure. I felt lucky she didn't yell at them to start making sense and also felt sorry for them. Yet, their faces brightened in the midst of such a heated debate. The conversations were like batteries that brought them to life. But those were their moments to savor. Not mine.

My mother turned from Terry and Richard's discussion. She saw a husky caregiver named Querishsa. Querisha was young and wore her tight black braids curled into buns near her ears.

"Well, look at that." My mother's upper lip rose on one side. "She thinks she is all special, with her thing in the air like that. Well, whoop-dee-doo." Her hands danced around as if she were speaking Italian.

There was no need for an incident where more vitriol was tossed around like word salads. I had already removed her from one setting because of her nasty comments and hitting, originating from her broken heart. However, I applauded her vim. She was thinking—and stating aloud what she was thinking. I'd found a place where she was no longer medicated simply because she could get angry. And no one within her new setting diminished her status. In fact, her feistiness only elevated her to near-queen rank.

"Miss Jean, I love you." Querisha's rounded stomach shook as she laughed and she went on her way.

After my father's death, my mother had fallen into a state of grief, an emotion difficult for her to articulate, let alone recall. She could describe a person or occurrence happening in front of her—*Move that thingy*—but not what was deep inside that connection, the *why* and *how*.

But my mother was coming back from the drug-induced haze that she had been put into only months earlier. I called it a haze because she had gone into hiding while the drugs masked her tears or joy. She was now teasing the caregivers and reacting to the conversations of others. My mother mistook a waiter at a café dressed in black head-to-toe for a priest and asked for communion. She nearly ate the plastic baby from the king cake during our Mardi Gras celebration in my home.

In those small, funny moments, I started to love my mother in her dementia. I wasn't always at her place to chat or share a meal, but even the hour or two I often spent with her brought a heightened sense that her awareness could completely disappear, so easily, and not even with her death, but with her disease. I needed to enjoy those interactions—the funny ones and those that stung—with her now.

Outside of the corridor named Boathouse Cove, plastic life preservers hung on the wall as decoration. We sat near the hallway's entrance, at my mother's treasured post, nestled into the navy blue cushions of the white wicker furniture. I wondered if the chairs reminded her of the carefree lifestyle of any Florida white sand beach, her favorite vacations.

I handed my iPhone with "Nice 'n' Easy" playing to my mother and sat opposite her.

She sang along to the catchy tune. *Nice 'n' easy does it* should have been repeated two more times but she went right in with "…every tiiiime."

She stood up and shifted her bulky shoes along the carpeting to dance. My mother didn't need heels when she had music on her mind.

I placed the headphones in her ears so she could hear the melodies without the interruption of the sucking sound of the carpet cleaner that a janitor was running nearby. She hummed along to tune after tune while I wished I had my pilot's license to fly her to Florida, right now, to stand in the light dancing off the waves from water that she presently feared. Finally, I stopped my daydreaming.

"Mom, what song is it?" I sat on the edge of my seat, ready to respond to her mood shifts at a moment's notice. What if she flung my phone in anger or protestation, or dropped it in boredom?

"Come fly with me...with your blue shoes on!" She jutted her chin out and laughed and laughed and laughed. Her petite frame trembled so hard, I crouched down in case she fell to the hard-packed carpeting and broke a bone. The crunch of a broken bone was a death knell for someone her age.

To a casual observer who hadn't heard her talk about my shoes earlier, her words wouldn't have made sense, but I didn't care.

"Mom, that was really funny," I said and let myself laugh a little longer at her joke.

"Oh, I know, 'Net," she said. The grooves in her face caught the beams pouring in through the windows, a reservoir of happiness for her to drink from later. And she smiled.

For the first time since my father had died, I wasn't worried about my mother clobbering someone, becoming angry, or getting confused. My mother existed in a world outside of me as her caregiver or daughter. She was making jokes, her sense of humor had been unmasked and for that moment, I basked in being 'Net and the beauty that was *Mom*.

That was enough for me.

A PROM NIGHT
TO REMEMBER

In which my mother
has some fun.

"Not this one." I fingered the long, black sequined gown and pushed hangers along rapidly as I scanned the other selections ranging in size and color, all donated by a local church: a strapless red dress, a green gown. "And," I said with a huff, swiping past another red, two-piece, low-cut outfit, "this, well, she would never wear that."

She was my mother. In her petite four-foot, ten-inch frame, she was rounded in the tummy. Finding an easy fit for an eighty-something-year-old woman's prom dress was a challenge.

But the bigger issue would be keeping her awake.

Her care home was hosting prom night. As an awkward teen, I'd loathed attending my junior and senior proms. I didn't know if my mother had ever attended a prom—but I did find a teenage photo of her wearing a royal blue gown, seated in a chair, with a boy dressed in a suit whose head was cut off in the picture. A former May Queen, she had never been in want of a date. But here, my mother was still a new resident, one in search of belonging, and I intended to create a night she could enjoy, if not remember, just not a night that included a low-cut dress that might show off a missing breast.

I scampered down the hall, nodding my head to the upbeat, acoustic notes of "Fly Me to the Moon" and "Bye Bye Blackbird" that carried around the corners. I was pleased with my selection for my mother—a long dress with a draped neckline, a gold lamé bodice and a long satin skirt that would make the rest of the women jealous.

But my heart sank as I entered my mother's room. She was resting in bed with the overhead light glaring down on her scrunched up face. Who let her lie down?

"Mom, I found something for you." I jiggled the dress on its hanger.

She opened her eyes and lit up at the luminous clothing and swung her legs off the bed to run her dry hands across its rough glitter fabric. It wasn't black, her standard issue color, but I sensed she was imagining herself dressed in that attire. I hoped she wanted to be that person for the night.

I heaved her up to her feet and a caregiver came in to assist in disrobing her. It was a task for two.

"What, what?" My mother yelled at me as I unbuttoned her green cardigan.

I ignored her and wiggled the dress over her hair. *Zip, zip, zip.* Finally, she was ready for her dance with a date to be determined.

But after the tug of war with her body and gown, she decided bed was a better option and lowered herself back into the crumpled, warm sheets.

Springing forward, I said, "No, Mom, you're all dressed." Too late.

I pouted. It was supposed to be a special night, an offering of time and music and romance. It was supposed to be perfect.

Taking advantage of her prone position, I clasped a pearl bracelet on her wrist and secured a necklace of small pearls around her neck, then slid a pair of black, sparkly sandals onto her feet. "Now you're ready." The caregiver applauded my deviousness.

"Yeah?" my mother asked in response to the clapping as her eyes fluttered closed.

Determined, I heaved her up to sitting and her eyes shot open again.

My mother's old jewelry box, stored below my bathroom sink at home, was filled to the brim with her clip-ons and pins. But I had left those jewelry pieces at my house and had new earrings for her—white rose clip-ons surrounded by faux diamonds—which I set around her ears. I returned her eyebrows to their former glory with a pencil, and quickly brushed lipstick I had found in my purse around my mother's mouth and pecked her on the cheek.

"Mom, come see," I signaled and she obeyed, surprising me. And together we took in the woman in the mirror. "You look beautiful," I said.

Our hands intertwined and together, we appeared as one in the reflection.

My mother stared at her image then led me to her wedding day photo on her chest of drawers. "Well, this too," she said. Her voice dropped from a cloying tone, the one she used with the caregivers she liked, to one more pining.

"That one," she pointed at a younger, smiling Jean. She understood that night, too, had been a special occasion.

"That one," I said, echoing her. "That one is as beautiful as you are now."

We paraded down the halls like Hollywood stars, me in my A-line dress, she in her gown. Memory still holds when a woman knows to clench her flowing hem from off the floor as my mother did, radiating light, aided by the reflection off the dress. And I radiated joy.

In the community room, blue streamers hung from the ceiling and swayed in the breath of the heaters. Pink and yellow tea cookies had been plated and platters set at each table with foil sparklers as centerpieces. I had asked my husband, Mark, and my skinny fourteen-year-old son, Davis, to join me and there they stood among the partygoers. "Most of the residents are women, who else will dance with them?" I had begged of Mark and Davis.

Strains of "Come Fly with Me" began. "Nana, would you like to dance?" Mark asked of his mother-in-law. She took his hand and they circled the floor, as he serenaded my mother. He was a better date than Sinatra because he was right in front of her. "We'll just glide, starry-eyed," he sang to her and she grinned. Some of the women spoke out of the sides of their mouths, envious of the lovely woman with such a handsome man. Her chest seemed to fill as she drank in my husband's blue eyes, never taking her focus off him as she moved her feet.

She danced only for the first part of the evening, but as she swayed with Mark, she occasionally threw her head back in laughter. "I don't think I've ever seen Nana smile so much," Davis said from the sidelines, cupcake in hand. I knew what he meant. Not since I had last witnessed her dance with my father at their apartment had I seen her shine with all the brilliance of an Italian summer sun.

When the disc jockey added a little honky-tonk music to the buoyancy of the night, my mother sat those ditties out. But one resident, Gloria—with a graying pompadour—rushed over wearing a cream two-piece gown. Gloria had her eye on Mark and together they trotted across the makeshift dance floor. "If that's your wife sitting there," she said to Mark in her raspy voice, "let's make her jealous." I pursed up my lips in a pretend scowl and Gloria beamed the rest of the night.

The evening ended in exhaustion. Mine. I was drained from my desire to find the right dress, the right fit, the right jewelry, the right song, the right way to keep my mother anchored in this night without weighing her down.

Despite the starch and icing in her belly after consuming three cupcakes, my mother walked with a bounce in her step as I escorted her down the silenced corridor to her room. She was up past curfew. Most lights were already out.

She slumped down onto her bed while I carefully unzipped her dress and unclasped the jewelry. "No," she weakly protested, holding a hand to one ear.

"There'll be other occasions we can save them for," I said. As if I were easing off glass slippers, I slid her glittering sandals from her feet and replaced them with her leopard-spotted house shoes. I knew how Prince Charming must have felt when Cinderella disappeared. I too felt like true love had slipped from my sight.

My mother rubbed her feet and sighed in relief.

"Feel better?" I asked as I flicked off the light on her nightstand.

"Yes," she said barely above a whisper, not wanting to wake up those who couldn't hear.

I spread the rainbow sheets across her body as the darkness blanketed the space. We kissed each other goodnight on the lips, as we had done since I'd been a baby.

Rounding the corner, I passed Valerie, an evening shift caregiver, on her way in to my mother's room. Already out of sight, I overheard the caregiver ask, "Was that your daughter?"

"Well, I don't know," my mother said.

"Annette's her name, right?"

I steeled myself for her answer.

"'Net," she said plainly. Her response was notably upbeat.

In past instances, her replies about not seeming to know me had stabbed me like a dagger to the heart. Not now.

This night, my mother had allowed me to fuss over her. She had enjoyed the heightened energy and attention while I'd stood as a fan on the sides of the red carpet, not telling her how many cupcakes to eat, but applauding the life she and the other residents had marshaled forth in those notes wafting around the room turned high school gym.

By morning, those memories had made a home in my mother's heart— and the lesson a home in my head.

TRYING TO GO FOR A DRIVE

In which I see autumn through my mother's eyes.

I checked the weather forecast: Sixty degrees. Sunny. It was time to take my mother outside of her living space. Not out there in the courtyard, but out there in the real world, the one that frightened her. The upcoming trip frightened me, too, because of her fears and my own insecurity over navigating public spaces with her on my arm.

I was planning to take her for a drive through the county woods or down the street in my suburban neighborhood that was comfortable, knowable. I would show her more of those colorful leaves she gushed about when gazing out the window. I wanted her to hear the crackling of those leaves and hoped she might remember how she liked to stand back and tell my father how to rake and pile and bag.

My mother had rarely held a rake. I couldn't imagine her long, slender fingers, which tightly trundled nut roll logs and other delights, wrapped around a rake. Her hands weren't made for the gritty pleasures of earth, but for heavenly delights. Yet, she must have jumped in mounds of oak and maple leaves, stacked high, when she was young. I remembered how she used to laugh, watching out the family room picture window, as all of us kids ran around in the backyard after raking the leaves into piles and leaped in.

Arriving to pick up my mother, I checked my back seat to ensure I had the essentials for a day out. I stored a package of disposable underwear, wipes and socks in my car in case of accidents.

Anxious to make our escape with the few hours of fall balminess available, I searched through the quiet corridors of a weekend afternoon and found my mother in the room of one of the younger residents, Danny. My mother was seated in his plaid rocking chair with her hair sticking straight up like a rooster's. Danny must have been watching football in the large activities room, but there was my mother in his chair watching a rerun of *The Lawrence Welk Show*. There was no cable connection. Someone must have pushed a button on a video player to make Lawrence appear.

"I have something better for you to watch." I scooped her upper arm into my hand and her eyes were near tears. It was rare to see my mother cry. Her sorrowful face caused me to cry, too, to rethink my plans of squeezing her into a schedule based on the weather. Maybe it was just her allergies. Regardless, I changed my mind about pushing her outside in quick fashion.

"We have all day," I said. "All day." She loved long drives. This would not be that. But she would be soothed by the slight bounce in tires along the smooth highways.

My mother rose and followed me, but only for a few strides. She turned away from the main door. She led, and for once I let her pull me over to the bulletin board with a posting of the October calendar, an "After Apple Picking" poem by Robert Frost and photographs of fall scenes. "News Center," she read out loud, drawing out *news*. "See, I told you." She turned to me, her eyebrows raised.

When she read, she wanted me to respond in the moment, to say, "Wow." Or "That's so good." Like a proud first-grader, she read everything in sight, the newspaper and the health department certificate over and over. I wanted her to keep reading. It was a part of her brain that still functioned. I couldn't let go of my mother, the reader, when her rhythmic voice had been instrumental to finding my own.

But I missed my cue that time. She yanked at my arm again and reread the headline aloud. Shoved me away. Stomped down her corridor away from the main exit. "Go on, you ridiculous thing, not a good thing." She turned aggressive. Why hadn't I praised her?

I watched her go, the back of her hair matted straight down, her once petite frame now nearly square, everything boxed in. Straight lines in a disease that was anything but.

Going outside was no longer a possibility. She was not in the right mood. I didn't know when she would be again. I was heartbroken. How did she know she was still alive if she didn't witness colors not seen in Crayola packs, smell the dry dirt, taste the aridness of a summer gone? Or hear the leaves crackle as they whipped around our feet?

I caught up to her, past a room where snores drifted out the doorway. She was halfway to her own room.

She stopped, pulled at her nylon pants legs. A female resident rambled down the hall, holding on to the wooden rail. My mother avoided her and twisted around, finding me in her sights.

I prepped for a duel and locked my eyes with her wet ones. Her pupils had grown smaller in size, more white showed through as if reflecting concern.

"I don't know what to do," she finally said.

I didn't have an answer, though I should have improvised. Instead, I approached and set down my large purse, lost for a minute, until a foul odor hit my nose. Then I sympathized. She had had an accident. They were happening with more frequency, sometimes thrice daily. Recent medications were speeding up her digestion. Or was it the disease?

We swayed like trees in the breeze down the hall to her room. She needed changing. There was no caregiver in my immediate sight. I could have called someone, gone in search of a nurse or aide, the way I did most times. I could have left this duty to the staff, but she was my mother and she had once changed my diapers.

I struggled to strip off her clothes, especially her camisole which she now wore after I had decided she didn't need her mastectomy bra anymore. I cleansed her body with a washcloth soaked in lukewarm water. That, too, didn't come without the heartache of knowing I was bathing the woman who had bathed my son…and me.

The corners of her mouth that had once turned up to form a juicy smile now pointed down. *Whack*. She slapped me on my head while I kneeled, something she had started doing when in pain or shame.

"Ouch," I said in a squeaky voice and scrubbed on through a short burst of tears. I had a sensitive nose, and a more sensitive heart.

When my task was complete, water dotted the floor. But my mother felt comforted. She caressed my cheek, wet from water and tears.

"I love you, honey." Her hand felt frigid to my hot cheek. A surge of electricity ran through my body.

My knees went limp. My name was not at the tip of her tongue that day. But *honey* sufficed.

She limped over to the window and I stood behind her.

Leaves of red maple shot up in flames against the eight-foot-tall white picket fence surrounding the care home.

My mother gazed at the sight with wistfulness. "Come here. Look," she said, though I was right behind her. She pointed assertively at the trees, her fingerprints smudging the window. "And that blue, blue sky." We marveled together for a moment. Then she began to count trees, "One, two, three."

"Three," she said again with pride. Out the window, streaks of orange leaves waved across her cheeks, replicating the colors waving in the wind.

My mother's job was complete. She walked over to the bed, sat down, and laid her head on two pillows. Her body was on top of the bedspread. She never napped beneath her sheets, as if preparing to rise at a moment's notice.

I put on a Sinatra album.

She nodded to the beat. "Ba ba ba."

Sinatra started singing. And she replied, "…under my skin."

He sang again.

And she answered, "…deep in the heart of me."

The call and response continued.

She could finish any sentence Old Blue Eyes began.

I tugged at the plastic shade to close it but it **rrripped** into itself at the top. Out the window were the colors no one could invent. So few humans were capable of translating such beauty but my mother had vanquished her fears and absorbed it all.

I cracked open the window and waved a green afghan over my mother's body. The fringed edge landed deftly near her chin. As I leaned down, her press of flesh circled around me, and mine, her.

Her eyelids were inflated from the tears she had shed earlier, but her pupils landed on me. I stared deeply back into her muddy, hazel eyes as she mouthed the lyrics of the song to rock herself to sleep. Propped up near me, her childlike face beamed. Not at me. Not even at Frank.

But at autumn's music, of leaves changing guard, readying roots for winter. Her face was lit with the last orange flicker reflecting the show in her mind.

"RIGHT THERE! LOOK AT THAT ONE!"

In which my mother develops a crush.

It was late morning when I tiptoed down my mother's hallway, called Country Lane, carrying a hot cup of takeout coffee. Dishes clanged in the distance. A bathroom faucet dripped. A wheelchair rammed into a doorway.

But where was everyone? Snoozing after breakfast? In their rooms?

"Right there. There she is," my mother called before I noticed her, seated in the corner, the dull light of the TV glare illuminating her round face as she grinned at me like an angel waiting to be beamed up.

My heart did somersaults. Her words meant *I know you. I missed you.*

Rain had swooped in across the outside world. But the three other residents in the room didn't seem to mind. Either they didn't see the dark shadows of a storm or couldn't articulate about their presence. Two snored and the other watched *The Andy Griffith Show* and whistled along.

"Hi, Mom, how are you?" I bent over and kissed her on the forehead, my lips tasting cocoa butter lotion on her soft skin. She was already washed for the day. I expected her eyes, losing their brown and green tones, to be sleepy, but they were alert, eyebrows raised at me, enough to wrinkle her forehead. Her jaw was relaxed and cheekbones unguarded. I could almost see into her mind, her struggle to name me into an existence that made sense.

"How are you?" she asked me and added, "Well, it's right there." She pointed. At the tip of her fingernail was a vacant magazine rack. No commentary. She wanted me to know it existed. She questioned why it sat empty.

"But there isn't any there *there*," I joked. No one laughed. Neither my mother nor the rest of the company understood the Gertrude Stein quote. Maybe I didn't either.

We nuzzled into each other and she ran her hands along the arm of my grasshopper green fleece coat. "Hey, I like that."

"You have the exact same fleece, only in pink," I said. My voice went up at the word *pink* to emphasize its cheery tone. I set my cup down on the end table and unzipped my coat. The level of heat in the place was overbearing most of the time, sending me into hot flashes at a moment's notice.

"Where?" she twisted her head around as if the pink coat would simply appear upon her request.

"In your room. Last Christmas, I bought one for you from Old Navy." I took a sip from my vanilla latte, caffeinated because I needed the lift to get through the visit. I kicked myself. She would not have known Old Navy. I was confusing her.

"Where is that?" She cocked her head.

Old Navy was a drive away, but her room was right around the corner. As I watched the water run down the windows, I let the topic slide away too.

"Hey, let me see that." She reached for the short coffee cup and clutched it now in her hands. She always coveted something in somebody else's hands. With muscle memory, she blew into the hole on the lid, sipped on the coffee and licked her lips. "Look at you. You have water on you." She brushed away a drop at the rise in my cheek.

"It's *pouring* outside," I said. Other heads in the room shook their heads and mumbled, understanding my tone.

"Oh no, my granddaughter doesn't drive in the rain," one whispered. Another typically nonresponsive resident perked up and said in our direction, "Not again."

It was as if the room came alive with my news about the weather. I took note of how important it was to bring my life, the good, bad and ugly, to them. How important it was to note this at all.

One of the caregivers that shift, Dominiki, wheeled a cart of laundry down the hall. Years back, my mother would have given anything for a laundry basket on wheels or one that magically transported grass-stained jeans to the basement and did the laundry itself.

Dominiki halted her duties for a few minutes to sit and chat while my mother stroked the caregiver's smooth arms.

"Hey, what's this?" my mother asked, referring to the tattoo of flowers and crosses on Dominiki's arm. My mother giggled. Then, out and out laughter came from a woman who often couldn't recite her name.

"Mom, you have the giggles today." I giggled too, like a child set off for recess.

"Oh, I do? Well, I guess I do."

Her bursts grew louder and prompted her to bounce like a character in an arcade game over to sit in the chair by the prep kitchen, the Chairman of the Board chair. She could oversee the food distribution, the medication dispensation, and the parade of residents streaming up and down the hall to meals or activities or to the tub and shower rooms and dining area. She lorded over the kitchen like a famed chef, drawn in by the familiar smell of coffee and bleach, morning and chores.

Frustrated, I hopped on over but there was nowhere for me to sit. "Do you want to walk?"

"No."

I cackled. The nurse, caregiver and other residents cackled and my mother fell to the edge of her seat. She was laughing mightily at her newfound authority.

When she ran out of giggles, my mother finally stood up and together we staggered down the hallway, squashing our stomachs as she read out the names on the doorways. "P. Swisss-ssshelm," she fumbled in pronouncing. "Now what is that?"

"It's Swiss-helm," I enunciated. "Like the head of the Swiss," I said and saluted her. Sometimes, my mother called me *You stupid thing* when she couldn't articulate her feelings. She was often right. I was stupid or acted stupid to redirect her. I was never the funny daughter, only the corny one.

She furrowed her brow and looked at me as if I were the one who had lost her mind.

"What is that?" She yanked on my arm, a sign to come up with a better explanation.

"It's an elm. Like a tree. Only it's Swiss." I slapped one hand on the other to make my point. Our hands held the last line of defense against misunderstandings.

She chuckled at that explanation.

As we walked down the hall toward coffee hour, she couldn't stop laughing. The caffeine now kicked her titters into high gear. I was embarrassed to be with her, fearful another resident, experiencing a less enchanting day, would strike out as she did to others. I couldn't predict what she would do in this state.

"What are those twirly thingys on your head?" she demanded of a resident whose hair was newly permed. The resident, mercifully, didn't get angry, and turned in the opposite direction.

My mother entered the activities room and made her entrance grand. "Participating in Meaningful Programming Moments," she read aloud while looking at the bold blue lettering on the professionally-printed sign on the bulletin board.

I'd heard my mother read that phrase before, about a hundred times.

The table of residents sat straight and listened to her. Unimpressed, they continued with their parallel conversations regarding the *Daily Chronicle*, John Audubon's birthday, goofy Dad jokes and movies that premiered on that date.

But my mother locked in on something at the end of the table. Or someone. "C'mon, let's go down here." She pushed chairs out of her path.

Four male residents, three of which were older-looking with sad, sagging faces, were seated around the far end of the table.

She motioned toward the decidedly younger male with round eyeglasses and curly hair. "Hey, look at that one," she said and moved in his direction.

"Shhh…That one? Mom, what are you talking about?" My forehead started to sweat. I attempted to reroute her like a traffic controller. "Let's read the news again." I handed her the newspaper.

Since my father's death, my mother hadn't taken an interest in males other than my husband, son, and a resident's grandson who arrived wearing a suit and tie and carrying a bag of Burger King french fries. She had only noticed him because she wanted his fries. I didn't know if love of any form was possible again for her. She had yet to make a friend or what

I considered one, let alone demonstrate attraction to someone else.

"You know, that one." Her finger pointed again at the younger resident, now beaming back displaying two crooked lower incisors.

My mother was showing an interest in a man? I blinked back the racy thoughts that circled through my mind and recalled my conversation with a female resident at another care home who had befriended a male in residency. The two had bedded down often in the afternoons, following the plentiful lunch meals. "Oh, my husband doesn't mind if I lie down with Bill," the resident had boasted. I bet her husband minded, but no one could stop the forces of human nature, not even time.

"Right there. Look at that one," my mother said as she pressed toward the end of the table, despite distractions all around.

"Yeah?" I tried to divert her path from behind and hid my grin in a pretend cough.

She turned and nudged me with her elbow. She raised her almost nonexistent eyebrows again, the ones now a rainbow over the light in her eyes deepening from a faint sherbet green, the color of the carpeting in our old dining room, to a golden shade. "Yeah."

We chuckled together like schoolgirls and a roomful of eyes cast their dismay upon us, hurt, left out of a joke they didn't get about an urge they all had once felt.

Moments that aroused the woman in my mother still transpired in her life. I couldn't stop them from happening. I didn't want to. What if my mother took to flirting with that man? What if he took to someone else? Those were questions for another day. Against the backdrop of an ordinary routine of TV, meals and coffee hour, the impulse to live was there.

My mother was there. *Right there.*

A SCUFFLE
WITH MY MOTHER

In which my mother and I fight for control.

S tuck between the hallway and door, I wrestled with my eighty-six-year-old mother, mixed martial arts style. Sleeper hold. Armlock. I undertook whatever maneuver was necessary to force her to go outside and expose her face to the sun.

My mother struck back with a whack on my behind, as if I were three again. It didn't surprise me and it wasn't really painful, only hurtful to my pride, which I had so little of left.

My mother and I were losing the war with her dementia. But when it came to forcing my mother as far away as possible from the front lines, I didn't plan to lose a single battle.

That day, my work had taken me close to where she lived with an hour to spare between meetings. From the center where I taught, I nearly skipped toward my car as the sun shone a glorious burnt gold in the one o'clock sky. That shade of season was also a sign the hours in the day would fade into nighttime ones and my mother would be left in the proverbial dark without the healing rays.

When I arrived at the care home to seek out my mother, she was walking out of her room, escaping linked arms with one of the caregivers. She wore a hooded, maroon sweater that hung down to her knees. Good, I thought at the time, she's appropriately dressed to go outside.

"Hello," she coldly greeted me, with a nod as if I were someone she saw every day, but didn't like. She was close. I set my stance. Maybe the caregiver had just changed her. She was always mean after having her clothes changed.

Her tone set my tone. "Hello," I responded in the same flat pitch waiting for more.

She barreled past me. Her pace picked up whenever she was angry and she made forward progress up her dusky corridor.

I chased after her like a squirrel, cutting her off as she rounded the corner for elsewhere, or worse, sunk into a chair for slumber. I halted near the exterior door.

"Let's go outside, Mom." I used my sweetest *mommy* voice. It was like tempting a child to walk to me by offering chocolate.

"Why?" she asked, and yanked on my denim jacket sleeve, jerking me backward.

Did she need reminding how much she cherished the sun? To use the word *worship* belittled her faith in the Father, Son, Holy Spirit and Mary. Still, if there were a Virgin del Sol to glorify, she would have done so. But adoration of the sun came to mind, akin to her dedication in baking communion bread and laundering the altar linens.

"You need Vitamin D," I said. And so did I.

Though her Catholic upbringing taught her otherwise about idols, the sun was the object of my mother's devotion as much as her faith. And I inherited that reverence. I had stopped attending formal church years ago, but dragged my son and daughters outside for long walks. We called it *outdoor church*. The sunshine always alleviated my physical and emotional aches and since I was practiced in the art of projection, I presumed it did the same for my children and my mother.

"But why?" she persisted in asking.

I elbowed the door open and lassoed her forward with my arm. "Why? To get some sun." Our conversation was now going around in circles with no exit ramp.

My jacket sleeve became part of a strange tug of war game for her. I pushed, she pulled away. I engaged and she disengaged.

And that was when she slapped me on the behind, as if she were paddling me with the wooden spoon.

"But I don't want to get sun." She used her angriest *mother of five* voice.

I ducked. My heart pounded as I waited for her to hit me again. But no slap came.

The alarm on the door went off as I thrust my hip through the doorway. The staff would come running. I needed to act quickly or she might turn on me.

"You love the sun. It's a brilliant day outside." Though my actions weren't positive, I tried to keep my words upbeat because other family members visiting their loved ones, as well as some caregivers, were listening in. I wanted to show I wasn't a bully. *See? I'm compassionate. And I know what I'm doing.*

"No, I do **not** love the sun." She wriggled some more.

With my toe anchored against the bottom of the door, I exhaled through my nostrils, swooped in and latched on again to my mother's arm.

How could I explain the change of seasons to her? As the colder, damp weather loomed, her time in the sun would wane. But she no longer understood the concept of a calendar. She tended not to venture outdoors at the slightest chill, not understanding she only needed to put on a coat or sweater. In ancient cultures, cultures not dependent on paper or electronic calendars, did elders lose their ability to tell time and season by the position of the sun? I prayed my mother might have hung on to hers.

I tried to swing her around into the path of warmth, warmth that would melt her anger or fear, warmth that could turn me into a puddle. If she felt it, she would want more. Me too. But she grabbed my pinky finger, twisted it, and scrunched up her nose and snarled.

"Ow, Mom that hurt." I pried my finger out of her grasp and elbowed her back.

"Well, well," she replied with little knowledge of the pain she had inflicted, or why.

I had to be the adult. I punched in the numbers to turn off the alarm, calling off the caregivers.

I stood in front of my mother and peered into her expressionless eyes. "Oh, Mom. I know you hate me telling you what to do, but just trust me," I whined and shook my fingers to get the blood flowing in them again.

Her eyes cleared like the skies. An unexpected, unarticulated epiphany. "Yes."

She reached for my hand and blindly followed in the direction of my voice out the door.

Breathing calmly now, I swerved around my mother's body several times, as her hand clamped onto my arm, and led her to where the sidewalk was splashed with sunshine.

"Oh," she said. "Oh, hey, this is something." Her entire being puffed up with life.

I pulled a nearby chair out into sunshine and she sat down. From behind, I saw the tiny hairs on the back of her neck, where the hair stylist used a razor, stand up at the slight breeze.

Relieved, she tilted her head back and closed her eyes. "That sun today is something else."

Yes, the ball of fire was something else. My mother and I were something else. Between those moments of loving and losing each other, we were opponents lined up on the same side of the battle lines. We were both something else.

My hour was nearly up. I stood, arms folded, in awe of my treasured conquest.

The sun's beams stroked my mother's cheeks, painting her face as a piece of art with her head dropped against the blue screen of sky. Occasionally waking to the chirp of a bird, my mother was glazed in a bronze glow.

I considered applying sunscreen to her head, since I kept a travel tube in my purse for just such occasions. But she needed all the vitamin D she could gather and store before the lonesome days of hibernating in the dead of winter.

As my mother slept, in her hand she clutched a glass of a strawberry sports drink. I wondered if I should remove it, or if she might spill it all over herself. If so, it would match her berry sweater. None of that mattered.

I would lose this war with her dementia, but for the day, I'd won a small skirmish. She, in the glorious sun, had won a little battle too.

In which I see my mother recognize herself.

W hat is music?

Truth (Kerouac). *Magic* (Rowling). *The existence of God* (Vonnegut). *The food of love* (Shakespeare).

What is music?

In the documentary *Alive Inside*, and in my mother, music is the self still alive.

At work on a novel about the impact of music on an old woman with dementia, I had followed the development of the movie. I also invested in the film through a web-based funding platform precisely because the topic mirrored my mother's life before dementia. I wasn't sure how much it influenced her life now, but I believed strongly in the film's message.

The movie followed Dan Cohen, a social worker, who played music on iPods to awaken the inner lives of individuals afflicted with dementia or other diseases, individuals whose existence limited them to a nursing home or long-term care.

My husband, Mark, and I attended a matinee showing of the documentary. I promised myself going into the darkened theater that I wouldn't cry. There were too many audience members who were probably the exhausted caregivers to a spouse. Some possibly even for an adult child.

But I wanted to know, was I right in sensing that the rhythms and rhymes of music helped people with dementia remember words or memories? Not only that, but did my mother create another world, a safer one, a braver one, when she heard a melody she could remember and claim as her own?

Scientists discovered patterns in a baby's cries that mimicked those of a mother's voice. From our earliest beginnings, the power to imitate, to repeat, to be moved was inside us. That was how music worked for all humans. My mother once imitated the classic songs of the Fifties, mostly, and now repeated the lyrics as easily as her ABCs. Through that repetition, she was moved because the chords and words were lodged deep inside her. The message of the melody she associated with another time, another woman.

I spent hours with my mother, seated at her side in her care home, where the strains of Tommy Dorsey, Billie Holliday and her beloved Frank Sinatra knitted a blanket of warmth between us. A dreamlike recognition glided over my mother's face and the corners of her lips turned up in a slight smile when she heard this music, whether she was at rest, sleeping in the sun or lying in bed. A recognition far more powerful than recognition of my face, or that of my father's face in their wedding picture.

It was a recognition of her inner self.

In one of the documentary's scenes, Dan interviewed a nursing home resident about her forgetting. "What is it you don't remember?"

The older African-American woman didn't hesitate. "I've forgotten so much after I became a young lady."

Dan offered to do a little experiment and played Louis Armstrong for her, and suddenly she remembered her son's sixty-ninth birthday.

Dementia, Alzheimer's, and other cognitive issues took many individuals back to the far reaches of youth's shore, but there were lost years that couldn't be accessed by a photograph, a spoken memory, even a daughter who tried her hardest with every tool imaginable to dredge up the mind's and heart's treasures.

Outsiders simply didn't know which years were the lost ones. Those like me ruled some out, speculated about others and used music to zero in on a few, maybe even to my mother's dislike.

If I developed some kind of dementia, and my spouse or children placed a music player to my ears, they for certain would play Bruce "The Boss" Springsteen, right?

But would they play ZZ Top, whom I heard live in concert at the Coliseum with my conservative college roommate, and we played air guitars to "Sharp-Dressed Man"? Would they play Robert Palmer for when my sister Laura and I wore little black dresses and posed as the Palmer girls at Halloween during my first year of living in Cincinnati and I knew then I was settled there, with her?

Would they select Joshua Kadison's "Beautiful in My Eyes" from my first wedding or "The Servant Song" from my second? Would they know, when Bob Seger's "Against the Wind" played, the song conjured memories of high school track, and from then on, every life challenge I ever met and surmounted?

Or would they play Sinatra as a remembrance of my mother and the times she and I journeyed together and separate, seated in the sunshine on worn wooden benches, each of us lost in a world our minds created?

Dan, the social worker in the film, established a worthy goal for a Music and Memory program where he placed iPods inside thousands of nursing homes across the U.S. I didn't know if his goal included places such as my mother's. And there were plenty of logistical challenges to that, yet centers across the U.S. were implementing the program every week.

Back at my mother's, I alerted Becky, who led activities, and the corporate nursing director, Jesse, to *Alive Inside*. After Becky studied the program and training methods, she secured funding. I was delighted to see the iPods in the hands of the residents and headphones over their ears.

Looking around the hallways, I noticed I was a bit young to be the daughter of a woman eighty-seven years of age. Most sons and daughters visiting were ten to fifteen years older. While I determined most visitors in their sixties and seventies were adult children and therefore more comfortable with iPods and other electronic devices, the spouses—the more frequent visitors—were not. But I was certain technology could drastically impact the life of someone with dementia. And the next generation of family caregivers, those who maximized technology and whose parents approached the age at which they might not be able to access music on their own, would add to the development of programs like Music and Memory.

The documentary lifted up the likes of me as I sat, grounded in my mother's reality, and selected just the right song for her. A CD player stood at the ready by her bedside for nighttime or downtime. One of my habits, when my mother didn't want to rise from bed, was to play Louis Prima for her because he tossed Italian phrases such as *Una notte abbracciato, abbracciato*—a night in your embrace— into his music and she was taken back to the square kitchen of my godmother's, the two lost in a country of their own making. My mother repeated the words, and understood.

Another unrealized benefit was how music in a foreign language reawakened another part of the mind, in particular for my mother whose parents spoke with her in Italian. I also played a little Mario Lanza, to throw her a curve. She laughed when I swayed at her bedside and crooned to her, *T'alluntane da stu core*—you go away from this heart of mine. Sometimes, she joined in the melody of her mother's language. I imagined that's what it felt like to swim in the womb of the woman who birthed you.

On my iPod, I created specific playlists for my mother, and made unwise use of music streaming services, which is why my data usage was higher than the rest of the family's. I played YouTube videos showing Frank singing with the Rat Pack, or videos with only Dean Martin and a drink in hand. When my mother visited our home, my husband cued up Sinatra on our sound system so that Frank was singing as she walked in the door. She was in a home that embraced who she was.

I couldn't make my mother's life perfect. Despite her best efforts when I was younger, she couldn't make mine perfect either. Sometimes, I neglected to make an appointment for her haircut. She had gone without matching crew socks for a few weeks because I'd forgotten until I arrived, and was too tired when I left to shop and return. She didn't drink grape-flavored Gatorade. "It tastes funny," she claimed and I showed up with the purple drink anyhow.

But the days we danced and sang and she bobbed her head to the strains of Sinatra were the best days, when I left her home weeping and beaming. I was so desperate to know that person inside her—that woman from the lost years who was not only my mother, but herself. And I was so happy, because in some small corner I found my mother, or she recognized herself as being whole in those half-notes of music. And then all of her was revealed to me.

As my husband and I re-entered daylight and crossed the street to our car, I was silent until pulling on my car's door handle. "Well, at least I didn't cry the entire time," I said to Mark.

The filmmaker's stories interwoven with Dan's efforts were heartwarming and heartbreaking. I cried with joy when Ben E. King's "Stand by Me" was played and Mary, a resident with early-age Alzheimer's, raised her arms up high and through the music was heard to say, "That's so big."

What is music?

Music is my mother's planet where she can orbit separate from her five children. A world she calls her own.

Music is a force of life that forces my mother into life.

BABY DOLL

In which my mother's hands find something to hold.

"Hello, baby," my mother said, soothingly, and her lips parted in a broad smile. The wrinkles around her eyes grinned, too.

The words, the phrasing, and the inflection brought back memories of the endearing tone my mother had used when she'd spoken to her children as babies, and then her grandchildren. She scooped infants into arms toned from years of scrubbing clothes on the washboard, and nestled them into the crook between her collarbone and cheek. When my son, Davis, was born premature and colicky, she rocked him to sleep in that position calling him *my little snuggler*.

But my mother hadn't directed the "baby" phrase at **me**.

Her companion caregiver, Bobbi, visited my mother regularly and treated her like her own. One year for Christmas, she'd said, "I got something for Jean and left it with her." Touched, I wondered what she had given, maybe cookies. But no. She had given my mother a baby doll, fully-clothed, dressed in a frilly pink pinafore and bonnet. My mother now wooed a twelve-inch, bald baby doll that rested in her arms.

The doll's fancy dress and blue eyes enraptured my mother. She dragged the doll everywhere. The bathroom. Outside where she often set it in the flower boxes. She also slept with the doll. The doll's clothes were subject to the washing machine as much as my mother's were.

She loved that baby. All babies.

Occasionally, I brought in *People* magazines to entertain my mother, as the larger print headlines were easier for her to read. The colorful spread and the sight of glamorous women and men enthralled her. Yet it was the cover featuring a celebrity cradling a newborn baby that kept her reading more.

"Oh, there, that one. Isn't he something?" she said about little Prince George in his prep school outfit with a whale on his shirt.

Another cover featured the singer Christine Aguilera holding her daughter named Summer Rain. "What the hell kind of name is that?" My mother squinted to read the words again. But she beamed at the photo of the baby with ocean-blue eyes.

Sometimes, with my mother seated at my side, I searched *Google Images* on my iPad using the term *baby* and displayed the matches. She was so absorbed in the nursery of photographs. She was overwhelmed. Speechless. Like becoming a grandmother for the first time. She giggled and could never settle on which image was her favorite. "That one." "He's so cuu-te." "Awww…"

Whenever I heard her say, "Hello, baby," for a split second I thought she meant me. But I was no substitute for her artificial, pliable baby. Instead, she swung her baby doll back and forth as she rocked in her rocker and peered into the doll's eyes. "You're so sweet."

When she cushioned the baby doll with her arms, other residents stopped in their tracks. If someone got too close, she whisked the baby behind her back and out of sight. Other residents marveled at the rare sight. "Boy or girl?" "Can I hold her?" "What's his or her name?" They spoke to my mother using a tone of jealousy and wistfulness. I loitered over the baby, feeling the same way.

My mother never responded to the comments, but I did. "She's a girl." Or, "She's about three months." Or, "Would you like to hold her?"

"How lucky," Mary Lou said and took off her glasses, amused, though she was quite lucky herself at age one-hundred to experience only moderate dementia and to be still walking.

"Isn't that something," a younger resident named Chuck whistled and rolled away behind a transport walker.

The doll had not been accompanied by a nametag but the name wouldn't have stuck. Her name was Baby Doll. That worked for my mother. After raising five children, and often calling one of them by another's first name, or worse yet, her husband's, she didn't need more names to confuse her. A generic term worked best.

One day, Baby Doll went missing and so did the doll's clothes. My mother was troubled. Though she didn't articulate it, she was restless, like a tiger caged, and paced up and down the hallways and in and out of rooms. She was upset, with nothing to carry, no baby to love. Most likely, one of the residents had taken her doll. Baby Doll was later found in the laundry, without her dress, but luckily still wearing her pantaloons. In the past, the staff had put out APBs for the doll and had discovered it toiling outside in the rain or lolling in my mother's plastic trashcan.

Baby Doll had a life of her own, reminding me of the latest holiday craze, *Elf on a Shelf*. We never knew where the plaything would show up. But Baby Doll had a purpose too. She was integral to my mother's care. If my mother had something to care for, she didn't worry about anything else.

"Put something meaningful in the person's hands," I'd read in *You Say Goodbye, We Say Hello: The Montessori Method for Positive Dementia Care*, written by Tom and Karen Brenner.

Put something meaningful in a person's hands. Sometimes it was a vanilla latte, or a snack of Fig Newtons. I learned not to complain about my mother's eating habits, unless she snatched a large wedge of brie cheese and tried to consume all of it, as she did one Christmas dinner. Food was meaningful in our family. And eating was a meaningful act.

In their stories, the book's authors mentioned other significant items: baseballs, violins, trains, pipes and wrenches (for a former plumber). My mother's fingerprints were all over my iPhone wanting to look at pictures or ask, "What the hell are you doing with that?" Her fiddling with the buttons was my excuse for the phone's improper functioning. When she visited my house, I handed her a wooden spoon to mix up a mean pot of sauce or bowl of sticky cookie dough and hoped she didn't remember the days when I was spanked with the spoon instead.

Since there had been a lack of new babies in our family, my mother welcomed sturdy hugs to occupy her hands. If no one else was around, Baby Doll was a substitute snuggler.

When this forty-nine-year-old baby rested my head on my mother's shoulder and asked the big questions about life, she cupped my cheek with her free hand. "Well, baby." With her other hand, she lifted her plastic doll high as if she had won a prize and was able to keep the doll at her side, something she couldn't do with her children.

My children were grown, living out of state. I knew that missing feeling and the importance of something meaningful in my hands.

A mother never forgets how to hold on to love.

Struggling to Be
a Good Daughter

WHAT IS FAMILY?
WHAT IS WORK?

In which The Game of Life becomes more than just a game.

It was Ash Wednesday. I entered my mother's care home with an abundance of guilt for not having attended to any holy day of obligation in years. "Three-ish," I was told by the receptionist when asking about the time of the church services.

I guessed there was no need to adhere to a schedule when time was all the residents had.

Wandering into the activities room, I spied fifteen residents, including my mother, watching a short film about the old Burma-Shave ads—"Dinah doesn't / Treat him right / But if he'd / shave / Dyna-mite! / Burma-Shave."

I recognized those ads, having used a similar marketing approach when I'd started a drive-through coffee bar in my twenties. I was still shivering as I took off my blue, lightweight pea coat—an outerwear mistake, since the weather had yet to turn—and recited along with the others.

So many factors determined the ease with which my mother, or any loved one, made the transition into long-term care a successful one. Mental and physical health. Were the surroundings made comfortable with familiar items (in my mother's case her Virgin Mary nightlight)? How often were residents able to slip outside into the sunshine of their own volition? Was the center's staff attentive to needs of an individual? And did they like to throw parties? My mother loved to throw parties and attend them.

But only one factor was within my control: The effort I put into making her feel as if she were part of a larger family that I had joined too.

Individuals with dementia were extraordinarily sensitive, like dogs that perceived thunderstorms brewing. If I felt connected, my mother sensed my comfort. If I acted aloof, she was agitated, and she disconnected from her surroundings.

My mother had settled in sooner at Arden Courts than I'd expected, with me coaching from the sidelines. She munched on bacon and ate pudding when she wanted, wandered outside spontaneously and attended community center events, including a viewing of her favorite movie, *How Green Was My Valley*.

She was herself with no restrictions.

But was I?

The spiritual director, Pastor Geoff, showed up at "three-ish" for Ash Wednesday services, after braving thinning snow squalls and close-to-zero wind chill temperatures. We both won bonus points toward our salvation that afternoon.

Peeling off his stiff coat, the pastor walked into a room full of willing and not-so-willing-(because-they-kept-forgetting) participants, to share in the glory of the Lenten season against the backdrop of crêpe paper Easter eggs strung from the ceiling and fuzzy bunnies positioned as table centerpieces.

With his long, knobby fingers, the pastor shook hands and greeted each resident by name. For the most part, he recalled the names of family members too. I glanced around and was surprised to discover I knew the residents by name as well.

We had formed a family. Sort of. It was a blend of workmates and family.

Workmates, because when I arrived to visit my mother, while the visit could be pleasurable, I never tricked myself into believing it would be all pleasure. There were many painful and embarrassing moments with my mother or with other residents, such as when Harold yanked his pants down and waddled into the restroom. It was work to feel what Harold could not and keep from laughing—at him.

Workmates, because I spent many hours talking with other residents' family members, swapping stories about loved ones who used to be garage mechanics or military officers who could still recite the names of their commanders. I was the sieve through which the essence of a loved one's life was distilled.

Workmates, because acquainting myself with the staff and their families, as they knew mine, was relationship-building, and relationships took intention and attention.

Pastor Geoff delivered an on-point, audience-specific sermon, and included a focus on thankfulness. He opened the floor for residents to speak of gratitude. Responses came flowing out of what a stranger might consider an invisible bounty.

"The sun and wind," a youthful Peggy said.

"Snow," said Harold, seated with his eyes closed.

Residents were still moved by the forces that existed outside of their bodies and minds.

My mother noted the peeling wallpaper border and a Mardi Gras mask hanging on the wall, leftover from a party. "That on the wall," she said with pride. It was her contribution.

One resident, Carmel, spoke out from the rubber seat of her transport chair. "Each other."

"That's right." Pastor Geoff extended his long arms as if scooping everyone into them. "We take care of each other. We are family. We are all family here." Balding and graying and sleeping heads nodded.

Family, because residents and loved ones looked out for one another. A great joy of mine came from observing residents, how they treated each other—a touch on the arm, a sharing of a cooked carrot, encouragement to walk to the salon with no idea where they were going.

Family, because other families offered my mother bits of chocolate or escorted her to her room, or vice versa, I helped locate the suede slippers of a family member's dad. My engagement gave help to the family who was not there, and also to the staff, attending to someone else in need when that someone else could easily be my mother.

Family, because I bought lunch from Chipotle for staff as a *thank you* on each of my mother's anniversaries of her move, and pressed dozens of the official family cookie, pizzelles, for her birthday parties—which included all the residents plus a Sinatra impersonator. She did not receive better care because I bribed the staff. Instead, *thank yous* went a long way in boosting morale so staff operated at their best for **all** residents.

The pastor made his rounds to distribute ashes. I brushed my mother's bangs to the same side as mine. With his thumb, the pastor smudged the ashes across each of our foreheads and my mother smeared the charcoal powder immediately after its application, sensing she was not quite ready to join the implied dust. I wasn't ready for her to do so either.

Following services, my mother settled back into her chair, reading and toying with the hymnal. I fixed myself a cup of coffee and, having skipped lunch, sat back down and munched on her bag of post-activities snack— Lay's potato chips.

Jack, a younger resident with Parkinson's disease, pushed his walker close to me.

"Chip?" I held out the bag and shook the contents free.

"No, I jj-ust cc-ame to ask if it's really cc-old outside." He stroked his scraggly beard and I sensed worry. "I d-don't know if my gg-uests will visit."

"I'm sure they will. It's not that bad, unless you're from Kentucky." My audience wouldn't get the joke that Kentucky drivers in southern Ohio were always cutting me off as I drove in the snow. He pursed his lips and grinned a bit when I spoke.

As a family member and workmate, I had watched a movie and sung with the sing-a-longs in my flat tone. I had also checked off church services to fulfill my yearly obligation outside of Christmas and Easter. I was productive and efficient.

Only one final item to check off.

I scooted my chair beneath the long table with its collage of colorful boxes of *Monopoly* and *Outburst* to play *The Game of Life* alongside Jack, and eased into my place at the family table of care.

ADVENTURES AT
THE BEAUTY SALON

In which I become
my mother's mirror.

"Can you squeeze Mom into your schedule today?" I asked the tight-curled, red-headed stylist.

Carol scanned her list. "I can do that," she said with a bit of a twang in her voice.

In my mother's care home, Carol washed, cut, colored and curled the thinning, fading hair of mostly female residents. She was in her early sixties and her role came with challenges. At a typical salon, women might have tilted their heads and sighed at the rush of warm water running through their scalps. But the women here feared the water as a baby might, forgetful, or unknowing of its power to cleanse and heal. And they feared the mirror reminding them of someone they couldn't recall.

"Matter of fact, I'll take her right now," Carol said.

"Now?" I hesitated. I wanted to be gone when my mother had her appointment. "But she'll take it out on me." I possessed full knowledge of my mother's distaste for the excursion she once considered a treat. My ears still rang from the last time I stayed. Water ran down her neck and she squealed, letting loose profanities even Italian mobsters would be ashamed to utter. My mother never learned to swim and the water was a reminder of how quickly she could drown.

For years, my mother had frequented the same beauty salon, A Touch of Class, in our hometown of Amherst to get her hair done. Occasionally, she toted kids with her when there was leftover money, or she tired of giving us home perms or snipping our bangs. In one case, when I was eight, she had my long hair cut short at the salon. Conveniently, I was then awarded the part of The Little Drummer Boy for the Christmas show at school.

My mother hadn't inherited the long, flowing black locks Italian women were famous for—or so I'd believed until I discovered sets of old photos from her childhood. Waves of black hair wove around her full cheeks. It was hard to know if her hair had been tied up in curlers or not, but I have no vision of her hair worn without curl. She chased after salon treatments and home solutions so often, I realized I'd never known whether my mother's hair was naturally brown or black, straight or curly.

In the evenings at our home when I was a girl, my mother would descend to the bathroom in the basement. Wafting through the heat registers, the smell of coloring dye and chemicals stank up the house and kept us from using the basement shower after sports activities. Hours later, she ascended the stairs with a new hair color and shape. Sometimes, the difference went undetected. "I thought you got your hair done," my brother might say. Other times, the coloring was drastic. "Wow. Mom. Red," one of my sisters would comment. She was trying hard, to save money, to still look fetching to my father or to herself in the mirror. I should have complimented my mother more. Yet, now in her dementia, I saw beauty every time she looked at me and never wanted to miss out on a chance to tell her.

In the past, when the weather had been rainy, my mother had covered her head in a black or red or gray nylon scarf and asked my father to drop her at the door of the church, Bob Evan's or school events. He had obliged. Whenever I heard or uttered, "My hair," I still conjured up my mother's same reaction, the fingers of her hands splayed out sparsely, desperately trying to cover her head.

My mother's hair gradually turned toward shades of gray, interspersed with threads of white. When dementia finally took charge of her mind, she no longer took charge of her hair. Weeks went by before she washed it. Her hair often remained disheveled, unmoving, glued down with Adorn hairspray, which I had thought was no longer manufactured, but my father had miraculously found a stash of it on the back shelves of Drug Mart.

My mother still made comments about hair but now they were directed at me. Her statements were derisive, but she was only returning the favor from long ago, when I had taunted her about how she changed her hair color and style to match the times and her moods. "What are those thingys?" she asked about my sweep of bangs curled just above my eyelashes. I cringed in shame. I now knew how she once had felt when my siblings and I had mocked her more original hairstyles and colors.

Carol and I led my mother into the salon chair. One of us stationed on each side, we released the chair support so the back of her head could slope toward the sink.

"Don't do that to me!" my mother shrieked.

I could see the whites of her eyes, and felt nearly able to detect the coursing of blood through the tiny veins along the side of her forehead. I saw a woman afraid. "Mom, hold my hand." I placed my palm over hers.

She slapped at it. "Just wait a minute."

Her words carried down the hallways and caregivers flew into the salon. Janice, one of my mother's regulars, called out, "I knew it was our Jean the Bean," using a nickname she had lovingly given to my mother.

I decided to hang back in the corner while Janice and Carol encouraged my mother to lean back in the chair. If they were trying to get her hair washed and styled along with being cut to please me, then I wanted them to stop lobbying her. At that point, I only wanted her hair cut—and to leave.

My mother repeatedly shifted between being happy and frustrated. "No. You're not going to do that to me." She pointed her mighty, mighty index finger at me.

Once again, it was my fault. And it dawned on me. Her dementia was my fault. Shouldn't I have seen it coming sooner? Could I have stopped the wave of her memories from washing out to sea? Not anymore than I could stop her from yelling now.

"Noooo," she screamed as Carol ran water from the sink hose and a few droplets splashed in her eyes. It was as if Johnson's Baby Shampoo had never invented the slogan *No more tears*.

I stepped next to the chair, and brushed my mother's arm. "Carol, don't worry about it. You can do it next time."

We all gave up on the notion of running water through her hair.

The stylist performed the rest of her duties the old-fashioned way, by hand. She wet my mother's hair using water in a spray bottle and clipped and snipped and buzzed and cut. "I'm sure happy you're here today," Carol said. "She usually gets mad at **me**." Her eyes stayed focused on her task despite speaking to me.

And I rolled my head to the side, thinking the salon was the last place I wanted to be.

My mother quieted down for a while, flicking at stray hairs that tickled her neck.

The scent of an herbal essence caused me to reach out again and massage her shoulder. "Mom, this is revenge. You used to scrub our scalps and held our heads over the stationary sink, you know, pouring hot water from the measuring cup." I remembered standing on the metal step stool, leaning toward the faucet with a towel around my shoulders. In my mind, I could still see the washing machine drainpipe in my view, the pipe's end covered with nude hosiery to catch the lint. Back then, I'd claimed she over-applied Tame conditioner to my hair causing it to go limp, like hers. Why did we always blame our mothers for our hair?

She let out a high-pitched laugh.

Soon, Miss Helen arrived for her appointment. An older African-American woman, Helen loved Etta James. "Helen, why don't you sing 'At Last' for us?" Carol asked.

Helen did and her voice motivated my mother to finish the line with "…a thrill I've never known."

The beautiful musical journey those two took together prompted frank discussions between Carol and me about how more music was necessary in the lives of the residents.

My mother nodded. "That's right," she said. And, "How 'bout that?"

She belted out a phrase of Sinatra's, now playing on my music player, "…I'll soon be turning that tide."

I imagined my mother as a thirty-year-old Italian beauty, waltzing with a strange suitor I had seen her with in a photograph from her California trip. Or, with all eyes on her, my mother dancing with my father in his crisply pressed pants at New Year's Eve dinner. She swayed to a rhythm not everyone could hear. Maybe those imaginings were more glamorous than her life had been, but it was all I had to hold onto, with my father—the story keeper—gone.

Carol wound the last of the curls. The spray pump hissed as she pasted her client's hair into place.

My mother squealed again and grabbed a towel to hold over her eyes, smashing the front portion of her styled locks. I wished I had a towel to hide my face, too. First the water, then the hairspray. She just didn't like the fuss that day.

The activities director passed by. "Hey, let me take your pictures, you two," Becky said.

But my mother was as restless as my dog when it came to pictures. She didn't like having her photo taken. Something deep inside her was never satisfied with what was captured. She was always hiding from the camera. "I don't like my smile," she would say. Or, "I don't like my hair."

My mother nabbed my phone before I could hand it to Becky. "What are you doing with that damn thing?" She slid down off the chair.

"I wanted to show you how beautiful you are," I said, holding her at arm's length like a long ago suitor.

She pushed me aside and stomped off.

I watched as my mother walked from one side of the hallway to the other and thought of how often she had changed her hair color and style over the years. I wondered if she'd ever found a look she was satisfied with. One that made her think her hair looked great.

As a youngster, I had teased my mother, but I never cared what color her hair was. She could have dyed it platinum blonde—or purple.

I admired and envied the time she'd spent fashioning her hair into various styles. I believed she was beautiful then, whether she'd trusted the camera or not, whether she'd trusted the mirror or not.

But she was more beautiful now.

In which I learn my mother is the real medical expert.

My husband and I had just climbed—and descended—a 14,000-foot mountain, Mount Kinabalu, in Malaysia, while visiting our daughter Shannon. Back at our hotel, we downloaded our emails from the states, twelve hours ahead of Malaysian time, while my legs wobbled and my stomach sank like the canyons that we had just crossed.

The first email I read was from my sister Beth, who also lived in Cincinnati. She had been tasked with overseeing my mother's care in my absence, and assigned duty as my executor should anything happen to me. It was now six hours later than when she had sent the email.

"Hi all. Hope you're having a good weekend. Just wanted to take a moment to update you on a few things. Mom had a seizure and is at the ER."

"What?" I screamed in the hotel room, confident I was heard around the world. My mother experiencing a seizure was dangerous, but leaving her care home was deadly.

Prior to my departure, I had snapped a photo of my overstuffed office closet shelves with the comments *Here is where Mom's files are* and *These are my personal files*. Beth laughed at the time. I did too. The last time I had traveled overseas, to Ireland, my father had been in and out of a rehabilitation center before his death. Beth was my proxy and toted my purple folder with all my father's medical information in and out of the hospital and the rehabilitation center. Now, the irony of me leaving again reared its ugly head.

"This JUST happened so details are sketchy. I am on my way to the hospital and can provide more of an update once I know more."

I panicked. Sweat gushed from my palms as I tried to type. "No, no, no." My husband claimed I sounded just like my mother. *"Just now reading this. We were on a mountain climb for a few days. Is Mom OK? I can't believe this happened while I was gone."*

Mark, Shannon and I had all been awake since two a.m., trudging up sheared rocks by three a.m. and closing in on the mountain peak by five a.m. During my climb, I cussed at my daughter for coaxing us into the grueling adventure and my husband, who moved nimbly ahead, for not waiting. I had no partner in my race to the sunrise. My only sounding board was the wind. Beneath my scant breath, I whispered to the slippery rock face, "Please let me return to Mom." She was eighty-seven years old and I wanted to spend any and all last days with her. We had always been two travelers on opposite bound treks across the mountain range of life. We were close, but not close enough. I had hardly fulfilled my duties or desires. Our journeys might never meet up.

Beth kept sending emails:

"Mom is fine, just fighting a fever now."

"Mom is fine, almost ready to go, but the hospital wants her to go to rehab."

In the hotel, again. Furious, again. My husband, Mark, covering his ears, again. *"What? No. They can't. They can't do that. Don't let them. She doesn't need that. She needs to be home."*

I spewed out the words before typing them. Someone with dementia could not be moved around like a piece on a chessboard. *"Who are 'they'?"*

"The doctors and social workers."

Those doctors and social workers were employed by a hospital near two long-term care communities specializing in memory care, one including my mother's. Why didn't they understand the consequences and stakes of moving my mother to rehabilitation if it was unnecessary? My mother knew her people. She knew her toothbrush was located in the medicine cabinet and she knew how to screw on the cap. Muscle memory. The staff had worked to train her.

There was no excuse for social workers and doctors who denied the rights and wishes of not only the patient and family, but in this case, the staff from my mother's home. It was a brazen and arrogant decision made to protect a hospital's readmission rates. They shuffled dementia patients like a deck of cards, and moved them to the next pile.

I felt untethered and could do nothing from overseas but encourage my sister to fight like hell. I wanted every family I knew to fight like hell and enlist the help of care home staff to keep loved ones in their most comforting, stable environment after a hospital stay.

In the hospital, it was reported my mother was crabby at times, fending off physical therapy. Strangers told her to eat soggy scrambled eggs and chewy sausage, and peeked under her dressing gown at the horizontal scar across her breast and the vertical one down her belly. She moved about easily and chastised more of the staff, putting on her combat shield as proof she didn't need skilled care.

The director and caregivers at my mother's home were relentless in their request she be returned home. Beth had battled in the same vein I would have—with mettle and might. The hospital finally relented.

I came home to the states. My mother was released to her care home. Both of us arrived home on the same day if I discounted time zones.

Every day for a week, I visited her to gauge her recovery. When I found her that first morning after my arrival, she was seated in an armchair, sleepy, but playful. I woke her and cuddled her like a newborn. We had a new lease on her long life.

I sat on her pink bedspread, wove my hands in hers and spun a few Sinatra songs on her CD player. Her eyes flipped open and shut like a music box.

The resident supervisor, Hallie, walked into the room. Together we sat on the bed while Hallie held a glass with red Gatorade to my mother's lips and discussed her new medications.

"I told the hospital staff, they should return her to our care." Hallie shook her curly red locks. I took notice of her buxomly chest as it rose and fell, envious, my mind wandering, as she retold the conversations she had with the hospital.

Becky, the activities director, dropped in for a quick look at the patient and, lowering her black-rimmed glasses down her nose, said the same. "I backed them up. Your mom needed to come back here."

The compassionate, wise individuals at her home had been all in. Why hadn't the hospital?

Each day onward, caregivers would track me down when I was in the center. It wasn't hard to do, given its format was laid out like the sun, community functions in the middle, residential needs contained along its rays. The employees were delighted—and relieved—to have my mother back. Surely, they would have dreaded telling me my mother had gone to the rehab center.

And each day, my mother wobbled down the hall and slurped at pudding or Jell-O or peach cobbler. Finally, she initiated movement into the courtyard to soak up the sun.

Her recovery came so quickly, encouraged by familiar faces and objects, and recognizable words posted on signs. She began reading, *Pull door until alarm sounds,* and *Mechanical,* and *News Center.* One night, returning home from a visit, I said to Mark, "Mom is so good. Either she is getting some great meds, or she is just happy to be home."

A week later, she was finally ready to launch into our trademark routine. It was summer. And a little fresh air was needed by both of us to reset our internal clocks.

"Mom, let's get up and go outside, ready?"

She didn't move.

Then, in Duke Ellington bandleader style, I said, "Uno, due, tre."

We repeated together, "Uno, due, tre."

Unsteady, my mother rose up and tumbled into my arms. I squeezed that little woman who had so much strength and resilience. She buried her face in my neck and patted my back, as if we were young again, both of us.

When I stepped back, tears pooled in my eyes. "I thought I was going to lose you, Mom."

She ran her hands along my cheeks, windburned from the mountain trek, and swiped my tears onto her blue, polyester pants. "I love you, too."

Unflustered in familiar surroundings, she knew what I meant.

She was home.

DON'T MIND ME, I'M JUST THE DAUGHTER

In which my mother responds to everyone but me.

One day, I asked my mother to say hello to a new resident. She flat out refused. "What do you want with me?" she yelled. Yet she posed with hands on hips and flashed a beauty contestant grin at a nearby caregiver, for whom she did what was asked, and immediately greeted the new resident.

I had grown annoyed with my mother, and she with me.

A few days later, on an evening during the holidays, she was sitting in a wheelchair in the kitchen when I greeted her with a quick, gentle squeeze. She could walk, but wheelchairs were sometimes used to move the residents faster than they could move themselves. She quickly stuck her chin out at my orange running shoes, which I had now graduated to from the blue ones, and crinkled her nose.

I looked down at her Velcro shoes, the kind little kids wore before they could tie their own. Saddened by the comparison of her shoes to mine, I inhaled deeply and offered another embrace, which she rejected again.

The room, filled with women sitting around tables, was quiet. Mealtimes were near silent affairs, as if the residents were fearful of criticizing the chef. "Hey, Mom, how 'bout if I roll you out of here and we can go to the party?"

"What party?" She creased her brow and wiped cornbread crumbs off her red, sequined sweater. She was dressed for a party she didn't know she was going to attend.

"The holiday party. Becky bought cream puffs and there's a new group of musicians playing."

"Becky? Who is Becky?" My mother threw her hands up in the air. Of course she would recognize Becky, even if she didn't know Becky's name or her position as activities director.

I didn't say anything.

"I don't want to go to any party." This time she kicked at my bright shoes. "And what about those?"

"Oh, you'll like this party," I said, trying to stay upbeat in my tone. I eased her chair away from the table, causing a loud screech across the tile.

My mother latched her fingers onto the table's edge. "I don't want to go!"

I bit my lips to stay in control. My eyes darted around at the other residents, their mouths open with interest, their eyes wide, like kids in junior high watching a fight in the school lunchroom. I had arrived at the junction where the redeeming moments happened with less frequency and the challenging ones more. My heart sank. Every time I tried to do right, I was wrong.

Becky waltzed into the kitchen. "Hey everyone, finish up." She snapped her fingers over the din of the dishwasher and the rush of the running faucet, the act of cleaning up a welcome noise.

I gave Becky a helpless smile.

"Hey Jean," Becky said in a high-pitched bubbly tone. She put her hand on my mother's shoulder and my mother gazed up and broke into a wide smile. Now that she had my mother's attention, she asked, "Want to go to a party? I've got cream puffs."

Becky licked her lips. My mother did too.

"And songs," Becky said.

"Oh," my mother answered and extended her hands toward Becky's and stroked her cheeks.

"It figures," I said, beneath my breath.

In an instant, Becky pried my mother's grip from the table's edge while I rotated the wheelchair.

My mother continued to hold Becky's hands, tugging at them ever so slightly. She inched forward in the wheelchair and arose like Lazarus while I stood in awe.

Once in the community room, where bells clanged through the speakers, my mother created a stir as she sought out an empty seat.

"I don't like him," my mother said loudly about a resident named Harold, who wore a patch over his eye and couldn't hear. "You're in my way."

"Hunh?" asked Harold. His question irritated my mother and I swallowed hard.

"Why don't you sit here, Jean?" Becky pointed to an empty seat out of sight of Harold.

My mother sat in the green seat indicated.

I was shamed again. My mother listened more to Becky than to me. Maybe she looked more like someone in charge. Or someone not me. I was envious of Becky's easygoing manner. Is that why my mother responded to her?

"Welcome everyone." Becky waved at the audience, comprised of family members and residents, some in wheelchairs, others with walkers standing guard nearby. "Welcome to our annual holiday open house."

The clapping was thunderous and woke a few residents already fast asleep in their transport chairs.

The middle-aged musicians of the Beechwood Trio walked into the room with the female musicians dressed in long gowns flowing across the floor and the males wearing tuxedos. As they played a steady stream of Baroque classics, residents sat straight up in their chairs, their ears tuned to the sharp notes and awkward pacing quite different from standard Christmas fare.

My mother's unpredictable outbursts punctured the interval of rest in between the music.

"C'mon, let's go," she shouted. She had left her seat and now tugged at a tall, lanky guest, mistaking him for a musician, as he had been standing close to the speakers. It was unclear if she wanted more music, more silence, a whirl on the dance floor, or if she was suggesting the two of them should leave together.

From behind, an aide passed around plates of cheese and set them at the tables. When my mother didn't receive hers because she was still standing away from the other residents, she hollered across the room, "Hey, wait a minute." Like a bratty kid, she wanted everything in an instant. Like an embarrassed mom, I wanted her to stop.

"Slow down, Mom." I cupped her elbow and led her to a seat, but I could sense her patience with me and mine with her was almost up.

The musicians strummed "The Highlands of Holland" and teased that there were no actual highlands in Holland. Some of the audience, including me, groaned. My mother flapped her hands in the air, frustrated. She didn't understand the joke. She watched me laugh and heard the chuckles of those around her. Her irritation was spelled out in the lines across her face.

She grabbed the sleeve of my green, puffy coat. "Lean here," she screamed into the space where silence had just been.

My cheeks lit up on fire. "I don't understand," I said. My mother leaned her head toward me and nuzzled her cold nose and cheeks into my face. Then I understood what she really wanted that instant was me.

Later, I led her back down the hushed corridors, last to go to bed. She wanted to sit in a sling-back chair that wouldn't allow her to stand back up with ease and yanked my arm toward that chair.

"Mom, let's get to the red door." I pointed a few yards ahead to move her forward. "And there's Becky again."

She pulled the other direction. "I want to sit." I honestly couldn't blame her and should have just left her there. "Well there is Mr. Red Door," she said, pointing to Becky but her words widely missed the aim of the subject.

Becky cleaned her glasses on her denim shirt and held out her hand, a natural fit for my mother's. "Boy, she really gives you a hard time, doesn't she?"

I flipped a strand of hair out of my scarf. My ears still thrummed from the harsh notes of the music. "Yeah, but it wasn't always like this."

Well, yes, it was when I was in high school. She pushed me and I pulled away from her. Now, the opposite was true. I was here way too often, telling my mother what to do.

I left my mother in Becky's care and near the exit door overhead Irma, a German-born resident, speaking to an older gentleman visitor. As the petite, white-haired Irma shuffled through the dimming corridor, she said. "'Vere ever tere is darkness tere is trouble. But 'vere people gather t' sing and dance, is good."

I thought of all the families that night whose lives also involved Baroque music and cheese plates. Those who danced in the light before leaving and were driving in their cars back into the dark.

The car was the loneliest place for me that night. I opened the door, got in and cried. It took a staff member of her care home to get my mother to go to the party. I felt inadequate, unable to control my mother's outbursts. Why wasn't I enough?

Then it hit me: If I needed the help of people who were not family—people with no expectations, like Becky, the musicians, and Irma—my mother needed them too.

BORN TO RUN?

In which my mother refuses to exercise and I learn to slow down.

"Mommy, let me run to you," my five-year-old self called to my mother and I ran full-speed into her open arms.

She told me, some time later, she knew then I was a runner and that storyline became a rallying cry as I ran track throughout my school years.

But while I had felt I was born to run, a reflection of my favorite Springsteen song, my mother acted quite the opposite.

One morning in the community room at her care home, I watched as she sat in a circle and repeated the words of an on-screen instructor calling out orders, "Up, up."

But my mother wasn't moving an inch.

"And up! And up!" A woman wearing pink leg warmers and a tight perm from the Nineties shouted from the video.

"Mom, raise your arms," I said. I approached her from the side and elevated one arm from beneath her triceps. I noticed her muscle was more taut than mine at the present.

"What?" She beat my hands away and refused to comply.

When I was younger, my mother had ridden her red Schwinn bike to our ballgames. The games were played in a wide-open space called "the fields." Those large plots of gravel, crabgrass and sand were the summer salvation of every kid in town. My mother loved to coach from the bleachers. She'd shout advice, hand out money for snacks, and ride on to the next kid's game. But she wasn't exercising: She was using a means of transportation to do her job.

My mother had also enjoyed strolling on the beach or wherever water washed up over her toes. She loved visiting Florida on either coast. But her strolls were taken to see the ocean, feel the grains of sand fall through her toes and to feel the sun as it bounced off the waves. They were more like leisurely lingers. In Ohio, she wandered happily along the stretch of the pebbled shores of Lakeview Park in Lorain, where she had once roamed as a young woman. It was the perfect length of beach for her to fall into a feeling of being alive—and out of the house.

Now, I set my purse on the floor in the activity room, speaking over the ebullient voice. "Lift your arms, like this." I demonstrated by flexing my arms and creating a crook in my elbow, raising my own fleshy triceps. "One, two, three, four."

My mother scrutinized my sweeping movements and crinkled up her nose.

"One, two, three, four," I repeated. If she counted, she might move.

When she and my father had visited in Oregon while I was pregnant, and gone on hikes with my husband and me along the rugged coastline or Douglas-fir forested trails, she had cut her efforts short due to *the wind* or *my hair*. She would often say, "This isn't good for your baby," after my son was born and we brought him along in a carrier, and she would take Davis home to babysit him instead.

She was essentially saying the same thing now. *This exercise thing isn't good for me.*

On many occasions, I showed up at my mother's for exercise hour. I sat beside her while the group, but not my mother, billowed a blue, green, red and yellow parachute up to the ceiling. Residents whacked at balloons while playing volleyball. I, but not my mother, tossed beanbags into a cornhole board and rolled a large plastic ball to knock down plastic bowling pins that didn't thunder when they crashed into each other.

I enticed my mother to attend the thirty to sixty minutes of exercise for the music. That's what I told myself. Music playing in the background stimulated, comforted, and aroused something in her, if not the need to release endorphins. And, too, she could sway to the sweet tone of Joanie, the physical therapist who led the program, and the inspiring voices of the occasional caregivers or the soft hush of Becky encouraging residents to stretch and roll.

Whenever exercise was on the schedule, I broke the cardinal rule of caregiving by caring only about what I thought was best and not what my mother wanted. I tried to get my mother to move, sweat, want more, do more, while she happily glanced around at other residents or commented about someone's coat—*Is that a...what is that?*—indicating a cheetah-patterned jacket. In general, she did everything **but** exercise despite being perfectly capable of following a simple instruction.

If I asked, *Mom would you like some chips?* and held out the bag, she readily thrust her hand into the bag with the precision of an archer or would instantly grab the bag and keep it on her lap. She threaded her arm through the hole of her sweater like a seamstress threading a needle, or drank her sports drink down like a college beer chugger after swallowing her medication if given instruction by the nurse.

She could lift an arm or a leg when it made sense to do so. But exercise never made sense to her.

My mother wasn't lazy. She had walked all over Italy with vigor and delight at age seventy-seven. She'd washed second-story windows at age eighty. But she wasn't into exercise for the sake of exercise. She was a purposeful walker, not an exerciser. She wasn't going to ruin her hair with sweat, unless the sun was involved. Out in the bright light, she could sit for hours, take her infamous twenty-minute naps as a break from nagging at her bickering children or wave to the passersby she might know cruising down our dead end street.

She simply recognized exercise for what it was—someone telling her to change who she was—and she refused.

On the video, the instructor flexed her muscles and called out, "Shoot like you are playing basketball."

My mother had played basketball in her upper school days. At five feet tall, she was the captain of her team. But clearly she differentiated sports from exercise.

The instructor on the screen was still calling out orders. "A what? Oh you're crazy," my mother said.

I refused to give in. I was here and we—she and I—were going to exercise.

The instructor shifted the focus to legs. My mother's ankles were swollen. I kneeled on the floor and gently swung her legs in time to the count. "One, two, three, four. One, two, three, four."

I remained deep in concentration, noting how the thigh and calf muscles in my mother's legs boasted of contours and not fat. I didn't want to lift my mother's legs too high for fear she would scream I was hurting her and call social services. And I wasn't going to let her feet rest low in case she stopped. Finally, my eyes caught some independent movement from her.

Her head swiveled around. Her body tightened and appeared ready to begin to exercise. **Yes!** But then I realized her sights were set on the post-workout goodies and her movement was purposeful: She wanted to walk over to the snack table.

"I'm doing this exercise for her," I said aloud. "Aren't I?" She was simply proving Newton's Law that a thing at rest stays at rest unless pushed on by some other force…such as post-workout cookies.

Charlene, an older resident still of sound mind, lifted her leg high as commanded. She chuckled but said nothing. A few residents peered over their eyeglasses at me. I must have looked ridiculous trying to push and pull on a grown woman's legs—legs that hadn't budged from her position on anything in years.

I plopped on my backside in my jeans and laughed too. I was exercising—for her. I was sweating—for her. I had wanted to do everything—for her. Perhaps I was still trying to prove I was the favorite. I guess that was my definition of winning.

Damn it.

Later that day, away from my mother and out for a jog, I had a realization. While I always exercised as a way to drive out my demons, my mother found other means by climbing stairs, carting loads of laundry or waxing floors. What exercise was to me, housework was to my mother.

I applauded my mother for fighting against doing things she found ridiculous and not giving in to what her caregiver-daughter-workout instructor deemed necessary. She now had only one way to drive out her frustrations of the day: Show her exercise-obsessed daughter that she was still herself and not going to do anything that didn't make sense to her.

I might have been born to run, but my mother had been running all her life, ferrying kids and laundry, chasing after grandchildren, running to the grocery store. The only movement that now made sense to her was a walk outside in the sun. And I was happy to oblige.

RAISING HELL
IN THE HOSPITAL

In which I learn to question the doctors and trust myself.

It was eight in the morning and I was typing on my laptop when the phone rang and my fingers skidded to a halt.

Before I could exchange pleasantries with the caller, the low voice of the nurse from my mother's home came on the line. "Your mother fell. We think she's okay, but we're sending her to the ER. Where do you want her sent?"

My day suddenly swerved and hit a dead end. Another incident that would leave my mother exposed.

Despite the sense of emergency, I hesitated and wondered. Which hospital **should** I send her to? During my mother's last admission, we'd battled with staff at one hospital to transition my mother back to where she lived and not rehab. Luckily, I had a choice and chose the other hospital.

Twenty minutes later, I stormed through emergency room doors where rubbing alcohol vapors filled the air. I nearly gagged. Emergency rooms were never a pleasant experience. I had far too many instances in my background with my first husband to prove it.

My mother lay in Bed Six, her eyes disappearing into their sockets. She acknowledged me by tipping her nose in my direction and let her head fall back into the flattened pillow.

She wasn't bruised...yet. There were no broken bones that I knew of...yet. The medical team would have to shift her around and see if she screamed to find out, and I didn't want to be in the room for that. The noise would be worse than the incessant beeping of the IV pump in the next bed.

My mother's attending physician poked her head in through the curtain. "Is this your mom?" The young, female physician whispered her question quickly as if she were in a hurry to finish her rounds.

My hands were still shaking from my race up the highway to the ER. "Yes, but you don't have to whisper. She'll sleep anyhow. What do you think is up?" I was worried about her balance. It was already enough of an act to keep her safe from falls and flu around other residents of the same age and immunity.

"Well, we're going to do a round of X-rays, CT scans, MRIs."

In other words, play the standards. The doctor probably saw me roll my eyes.

She let go of the blue curtain and disappeared into the murmur and blinking and bleeps of the emergency room.

Oddly, the doctor hadn't said another word. Though my mother's medical data had been entered in the system from another visit, the doctor never asked for additional information regarding her condition. To be honest, I didn't push it. The day had broken me and my mind had shut down.

By late evening, the administrator assigned my mother to the neurology-trauma-orthopedic floor. When a patient was assigned to a floor with three names, that meant the doctors really didn't know what had happened.

After my mother was unsettled and resettled into her room, I kissed her goodnight. "I think you'll just be sore in the morning," I said to her as she dozed. "We'll be back to our usual in no time." I was confident she could hear me in her dreams, or nightmares, and began to rub her feet.

Throughout the night, I bunched up the covers in my own bed and threw them off. I wrestled with the sheets as if fighting off a bear, like my mother used to say. My mind wandered to places it shouldn't go at night. Concussion. Stroke. And always, after one of my mother's incidents, I scrutinized her level of engagement and asked, *Where was she on the continuum of forgetting?* and answered, *Half-way there, wherever there might be.*

The next morning at dawn before the doctors rounded or the churchwoman came by for communion, I nudged my mother's shoulder and nestled my nose into her neck. I was certain she could feel my warm breath. Her eyes opened and gleamed but her speech was slurred. "Helll… oooo."

Lying in her bed with her head elevated, she shrank beneath the glare of hospital lights, a wounded animal.

"Breakfast?" I asked and she nodded, opening her mouth as I spooned in soupy oatmeal and canned peaches. The runny fruit fell back out.

She tried to catch the runoff with her hand but when she moved, she groaned. "Oh. Oww."

"Knock, knock," someone said from the doorway. Thin and with a mop of brown hair, the in-house orthopedic doctor introduced himself. "Hi, I'm Doctor O."

I took up my invisible sword and shield. "Hello, I'm Jean's daughter." I held out my hand but he went right ahead and rinsed his hands with Sterisoap and ignored my gesture.

"No broken bones found. So you want to tell me what happened?" He snapped on rubber gloves, pressed on her body in a few areas and flipped the gloves off.

While he viewed reports on the computer, I retold what I knew of the story. She'd been living at her care home for three years. She had fallen. Yes, she was normally ambulatory. Yes, she had moderate dementia.

"Well, I've looked at her tests and don't see fractures. You know she's old, and may have decided it's time to check out." His eyes stayed focused on the blinking screen.

I shook my ears, where shower water still sloshed. Was that his diagnosis just because she was sleepy? Suicidal? Giving up? I didn't care about titles on badges. "Sure, she fell, but she's not *checking out*." I said this loud enough for my mother to hear, despite her falling back into slumber.

"She may have to go to skilled care. For now, we can get PT in here, see if that helps, but this may be where she's at."

My mother wasn't **at** anywhere, except for a hospital. She was right in front of the medicine man and he refused to look further.

I didn't waste my breath on why rehab facilities didn't always work for someone with dementia. I had been through this routine before. I wanted to shove him out the window but he flew out of the room to respond to a page instead.

An hour later, the internist rounded. After our introductions, he offered his own misinformed assessment without making eye contact with my mother or me. That would not have sat well if she had been aware. "I didn't see signs of anything broken," he said. "She's been less alert"—*when had he seen her?*—"than I would expect. I guess in the ER they gave her narcotics."

"They did?" I asked, alarmed. "But I was with her the entire time. Are you sure?" I questioned the young but balding authority figure. I could feel the coffee churning in my empty stomach. The temperature in the room and in my blood began to rise.

He rustled my mother's sheets and listened to her heart with his scope. "Yep, the ER doc told me she was given morphine. That's why she's out of it."

"What? Can you look it up again?" I uncrossed my legs, ready to rise. "They're not supposed to do that without my consent." If I had to examine the charts myself, I would hack into their system and do it.

He raised an eye at me, reluctant to take advice from a five-foot tall woman wearing orange sneakers. The doctor turned toward the computer and peered over his reading glasses. "Here it is, no, wait. No, it's probably on this screen…I guess she didn't get pain meds."

"You **guess**?" I curled my lip like a teenager.

"I thought ER told me they gave her pain meds. But, oh, well." He switched off the screen.

Oh, well? I knew more than they did. "What does it say about her blood work? Her loopiness makes me think she has a UTI." How could he not hear the rage in my voice?

"Or, it could just be because she is old and confused," the doctor said.

Did he just say that? There was truly an epidemic of misinformation among doctors in the hospital. I felt like I was in a boxing ring and some invisible force, possibly the woman in the bed, was urging me on.

"Let me check." He flicked the screen back to bright. "Ah, yes. A UTI. Antibiotics were ordered this morning."

He saw my smirk. I didn't care. I had seen beneath his charade. What if I hadn't been there to grill him? What would he have prescribed for my mother or missed, based on his lack of knowledge?

The hospital clearly needed to educate staff on how their employees evaluated aging patients. Plenty of doctors prolonged life through unnecessary treatments, but when faced with the prospect of administering to an elderly woman with compassion, they lost interest in dispensing the right kind of care or showing any kindness at all.

I would not fight for my mother's last breath. She had experienced too many incidents in which I found her to be vulnerable with her quality of life slipping away.

But I would fight for her dignity.

She returned to her home surrounded by those who loved her and could map her medical chart like the back of their hands. And I sent a letter to the hospital informing them of their doctors' misdeeds.

Two minutes. If those doctors had taken two more minutes to understand my mother's background, researched her history, or just sat in her presence, they would have seen her as human. They would have seen her as I did.

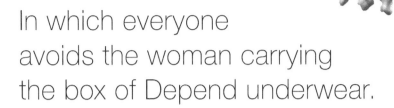

DRAMA AT WALGREENS

In which everyone
avoids the woman carrying
the box of Depend underwear.

I nside Walgreens, I scooped up two large, green boxes and cradled them between arm and waist as I looped through the overstuffed aisles of the store. The boxes were weightless but I struggled to hang on to the other items in my arms: Gatorade, lipstick and several bottles of body wash. I exhaled deeply, waiting my turn in the checkout line for an older, gum-snapping clerk deep in concentration. I could feel the scrutiny of folks standing ahead of and behind me, gaping at my packages.

I glanced down, nudged up the collar on my raincoat with my chin, then stared at a cover of *People* magazine with Angelina Jolie on the front. Finally, I silently read the marketing label on the box of disposable underwear: *Now boasting of more confidence.*

But not for the person making the buy.

Standing there, I recalled the Sundays in my youth when I stood awkwardly with my father in line at a different drug store.

Every Lord's Day at home had started with my father's brusque voice waking us up. He threw the bedspreads off our pretending-to-be-sleeping bodies. We were called to participate in the forced march to church for which we would attain a heavenly reward—Perkins' fluffy pancakes loaded with strawberries and whipped cream. The bribe softened the blow of the obligatory trip to the Catholic cemetery to pay homage to our ancestors.

By noon, my father had a few more errands to run. He drove to Willow Hardware for garden twine and checked on the family's shoe business. The store closed on Sundays but he made certain no one had broken in, or confirmed the cash drawer was ready for Monday. When he completed those tasks, he made what came to be known as the "Drug Mart Run."

I was a seventh-grader and in quite the dilemma on Sundays. Should I ride in the Suburban with him or not? The choice involved accompanying him to the shoe store and possibly convincing him I had grown out of my last pair of Thom McAn clogs, despite having always worn the smallest size in the store, and thus getting a new pair. However, if I went along, I also had to go with him to Drug Mart.

It was an either-or proposition.

My father slipped a sloppily-written list for Drug Mart in his pocket. The list contained Ivory Soap, picture hangers, shaving cream, or whatever else my mother had forgotten to buy during her weekly grocery shopping. The list also contained something else. He shook his head when he read the additions of tampons, mini pads and maxi pads in one daughter or another's quickly-scrawled curly handwriting at the bottom of his list.

If I accompanied my father, I was met with stares from customers in the checkout line who I figured were silently asking, *Is she old enough for a period?* Or I stood next to my father while he paid for the tampons or worse yet, while I lugged the package of pads around and I pictured people imagining me having my period. Might as well tell the world.

As a preteen, I never considered my father knew all too well about periods, despite my mother's six pregnancies and raising four girls in the home. Save face or shop for shoes? That was my only consideration. Often, I chose to stay at home and wash the other cars, another Sunday chore, and hope he brought home the right kind of tampons or pads.

Now in Walgreens, I felt a humiliation that ran deeper than the embarrassment of my youth, this time because of my mother.

All the customers were there with a malady to remedy. Woman with Kleenex and cough drops (child with a cold at home). Tall, burly man with two boxes of Milk Duds (candy addiction, trying to break cigarette habit). Young gal with heavy eyeliner (small, pale eyes she wanted to enlarge). Me with a box of Depend Fit-Flex (mother unable to control her body's outputs).

In Walgreens, I was no longer mortified buying pads or tampons. They were part of everyday life despite my wish to be rid of the added expanse to my waistline and expense to my wallet. But my face blushed as I whisked the large boxes of disposable underwear onto the counter. Ahead of me in line, a thirty-something male customer built like a lumberjack with a chiseled jaw smiled at me as if to say, *What a pity. You're incontinent.*

My mother's body no longer functioned as mine. She soiled her sheets and sometimes, urine or excrement dribbled all the way down her legs and her shoes had to be thrown into a washer that sucked the air from the cushioning of the insoles. *Did you know that?* I wanted to shout at the patrons, feeling as if a period had just soiled my white pants in junior high school. *Did you know this could happen to you someday?*

Beneath my shame about my mother was also a woman who wanted to scream, *These are not mine! They're for my mom! She's in a memory care home!*

But why would the lumberjack believe me when I also juggled a tube of lipstick in my mother's favorite color and a *People* magazine in my arms, alongside a scented candle (gift for dog-sitter), shoelaces (my Nike nylon ones always slipped from their knots) and sports drinks. What kind of elderly person drank sports drinks? Or tied her own shoelaces?

I swiveled my head and pled my case silently to those behind. Their faces offered no relief.

The option existed for my mother's care home staff to order the in-house brand of disposable underwear. I once did the calculations and figured I could save actual cents and my mother's fashion sense by purchasing the disposable underwear at Walgreens instead. She would have the best of whatever I could make happen for her. If that meant disposables that looked more like underwear and were manufactured in a delicate peach color, my mother would have them.

I shoved the boxes toward the register and the clerk's grim face relaxed. She looked at me with a show of mercy seen only by a priest after confession. "Do you have your rewards card?" she asked in a grandmotherly voice.

"Of course I do. I always use it when I come in here for my **mom.**" I wanted the surrounding customers to hear me. I begged for the rugged Paul Bunyan, slipping money and receipts into his wallet, to look at me with admiration and see the great lengths to which I went to please my mother.

Instead, he went on his way and I scurried off too, conscious of customers in the parking lot who might also get the wrong idea as I grappled with boxes that weren't mine.

I didn't need pity from the other customers. I directed plenty of that toward my mother. And it was clear each patron had his or her own burden to bear. However, in the future, I planned to reward myself with pancakes when my tasks included buying disposable underwear. And I would buy new shoes for my mother whenever she needed them, a prize for her having to wear a fading sense of fashion and pride.

STILL SAVING HER A SEAT

In which
two residents
fall for each other.

A resident named Big Pete edged his padded, green conference chair closer to the empty chair next to him. It was balloon volleyball time in the care home, boisterous with energy that day, and he held a blue balloon in his hands ready to serve.

My mother and I took our seats near the courtyard door while other residents walked or wheeled in, anxiety written on their faces as they angled for a place to sit for an activity they didn't know anything about.

Another resident named Robert rapped on his legs and approached the vacant seat.

"Saving this for someone." Big Pete's burly voice carried out both doors to the outer halls, refusing to let anyone sit in the empty chair.

It was true. He was saving that seat for Emma. But Emma wasn't there that day.

Emma, with her hair cut in a white, youthful bob, was a lively resident who lived down the hall from my mother. Always upbeat, Emma never stopped chatting, meandered the path at the former Blue Ash airport next to where her sister lived and waxed poetic with anyone who listened to the stories she told about her rebellious youth and sneaking off to the Albee Theater for adult shows.

Rumor was, after Emma's husband had died, she had a crush on a neighborhood guy named *Peter,* someone younger than her. Then her family admitted her to the memory care home.

When Emma arrived at her new place of residence, she was soon discovered seated in the west side parlor alongside Big Pete—ironically bearing the same name as her younger beau. The two found joy and laughter in each other's company as they peeped out the windowpanes to watch the birds or the residents pushing walkers to see who was more active that day, or interacted with guests and staff or anyone else who embraced them as a couple.

Stepping through the secure doors, visitors were immediately met by the duo. Oftentimes when I entered, I gravitated toward Emma and Big Pete and gave them a hug, a laugh or a *Where have you been?* joke to turn the tables on their lives and mine.

Their presence brought an unusual lightness into a space already filled with long stretches of windows. In my memory, Big Pete was always seated on the chair and Emma on the love seat. The sight of them lifted me and gave me hope that a relationship, even if it wasn't a romantic one, was not out of reach for my mother in her later years.

It was as if the two had already shared a lifetime together.

Both residents possessed moderate cognitive impairment. For the caregivers and staff who managed far more difficult cases and loved each person for who they were, individuals like Emma and Big Pete were subtle reminders of the lives residents used to lead.

Emma and Big Pete were also tokens of how surprising and impactful love could be.

Their joy in each other was evident, palpable, such that I often sat with my mother in their company to revel in their bliss, hopeful it might rub off on me, or my mother.

Theirs was the purest form of love.

Emma had found joy in someone and didn't care about his prior profession or his mussed up hair or how ambitious he had been. Big Pete had discovered delight without knowing how many children Emma had. Neither knew where the other one was born, raised or went to high school—which is how Cincinnatians introduced themselves—or what or who was important to them. Some topics rose to the surface and soon were let go.

The only topic each remembered was love.

As the balloon bounced from arms to hands or legs, my mother got up from her chair and rattled the doors and windows. She was always trying to escape. I let her go and spied on Big Pete seated behind his walker. He was telling "Dad" jokes to anyone who would listen. "Did you get a hair cut?" someone might ask him. And he would answer, "No, I got 'em all cut."

To his left, two chairs still sat empty beside his. Though no one was in his vicinity, Big Pete reached over to the chair closest to him and tilted the chair on its back legs, again eliminating the prospect of anyone else sitting in that chair.

It was only after volleyball and after my own absence for several days that I learned about Emma's sudden disappearance. Her son had moved her elsewhere. This was an event that occurred when the money ran out, when siblings fought, when any number of other circumstances occurred. But never when the resident was ready to go.

Now I better understood Big Pete's actions. For the duration of the match, he had held tight to the sleek arm of that chair, playing one-handed in a game with an invisible opponent that had a long reach.

It was Emma's chair. It would stay empty. A reminder to me of how brief and fragile unions could be, and yet still be profound.

WHAT IT MEANS
TO BE GOOD

In which
I find out
I am enough.

My mother and I exchanged dozens of letters during my college years. Her letters were like a virtual tour through her day, waiting on the painter, the washer repairman, another child about to return home.

The letters, two or three pages, front and back, were written in her precise, slanted penmanship despite a former teacher of hers who once had said, *Your writing will never be any good*, because my mother had paused between each letter of cursive. Little did the teacher know that was my mother's way of checking herself. She was always careful as to what she revealed.

She sometimes had mentioned my father in her letters to me, and filled the other spaces with the comings and goings of my siblings. She closed each letter with her standard lines.

The 3 B's, she called them. *Be Careful. Be Studious. Be Good.*

In college, I was a wanderer. My mother knew I might take off for a jog to clear my mind, early morning or late at night. Her *Be Careful* admonition was directed at me, at all girls really, as campus rapes were not unheard of even then. *Don't go for a run alone. Always go out with friends.*

The *Be Studious* directive had been part of my mother's child-rearing vocabulary for many years. Though I wasn't perfect in my studies like my younger sister Beth, I was industrious and my efforts eventually showed. Calculus class in college had been difficult. Beginning programming classes were a challenge for me as I learned new systems on mainframe computers, and I spent long hours in computer labs where most of my classmates were male. While I struggled to be studious, I relished the freedom campus had provided for me. It was a respite from family life back home and I eked out a computer degree and a successful career thereafter.

The *Be Good* reprimand puzzled me. There were no clear-cut guidelines my mother offered in her letters on how to do so. Of course, *Be Good* was the last line my parents uttered as they walked out the door and left us with the oldest Dover neighbor girl to babysit and referee us. They said *Be Good* in later years, leaving us home alone without oversight, but with clear plans to throw a party in the basement the minute they left the house. But in college, what did she mean? No sex? No drinking? What did it mean to *Be Good*?

My siblings and I fell into categories that fit or defined who we were for decades.

My older sister, Laura, had been the beautiful little girl, the artistic and endowed one. My mother signed her up for tap lessons, baton, Girl Scouts, flute and piano lessons, and beauty pageants. I overhead my mother on the phone, telling her friends, "She is talented. She's so creative." And she was.

But by high school, Laura had become a rule-breaker in my parents' eyes. She wore too many coats of mascara, changed too often into higher heels to match her bellbottom jeans. *Damn it, we'll be late for church* came out of my father's mouth as the rest of us waited. Laura stayed out past curfew and smoked cigarettes, breaking the rules for the rest of us. She streaked mascara across the dresser top doily, and my mother let her have it. *All you do is primp.* The term was used as damnation in our home.

My older brother, Paul, was into sports. My sister Beth possessed intelligence far superior to mine and the baby, Jeanne, was fun-loving and stubborn. I was squeezed in the middle. There was little room to do anything except what I was told. To avoid my father's wrath, I chose to *Be Good*. To avoid my mother's derision, I chose to *Be Good*.

Reading my mother's letters, I often asked myself, *Haven't I already been good?*

As a child, I had given back to my parents in service of any kind, trying to *Be Good*. I worked hard to elicit one long, drawn-out and cheek-caressing moment from a mother who would say *You're so good* if I folded the piles of my father's work clothes on the laundry room's green speckled table, or if I swept every blade of grass off the sidewalk after my father cut the lawn.

When I went away to college, I fled my hometown without a single desire to look back. I left behind a father who had lost his livelihood through the dissolution of the family shoe business. The entire Januzzi side of the family disintegrated like the last vestiges of a leather upper sole. I watched Beth lapse into an eating disorder and Jeanne rebel for being left at home with an unspoken and misunderstood misery.

My mother was often angry with me for wanting my independence. She wrote, *Deep down inside, I feel a little hurt that you are so independent. My little girl doesn't need me. But it is for your own good that you are that way. I am very proud of you. Being the middle child has worked to your advantage.* But my independence was really shame in disguise. It was devastation over watching the world I thought I had known crumble. The town had grown smaller with talk of my family's loss of our business and I felt a shame about the gossip, about the money problems I perceived my parents to have. My mother accused me of returning home on weekends as an angry young woman. She was hurt that I saw the family through a different lens. And she was used to me being the good kid. *I thought you were supposed to grow up at college, but instead you come home and act entitled, and disappointed at us.* She was right. But didn't she know how hard the separation for me had been as well?

The world had not turned in the direction I had expected.

After the closing of the family shoe store our life as the Januzzis no longer followed form and my only outlet to express that at the time—because I could not name that which had not been named by my parents—was to strike out at my mother.

My father braved the private and public humiliation of the store's closing, and my mother too. But they went on: They took golf lessons. They were learning computer skills. They were growing.

I had spent my childhood living in the shadow of my taller sister, with a bigger personality and brightly-lit, wide eyes and round face that matched my mother's. When my mother saw me, she saw the face of her own stern mother, features hardened, more cheekbone, less cheek, less delicate than her own. Even in birth, I was a bit of an afterthought. The world had introduced me as a boy through a mistake in the local paper. My father phoned in to correct the birth announcement.

Yet my mother saw me as good. *Good.* That's what she had told her friends over the phone. Of course, there were times in college when she had called me anything other than *good.* And there were times too many to count (and numerous high school and college friends who might reveal otherwise) when I was not. But *Be Good* stuck in my head and became a common refrain in my life. I understood *Annette follows the rules = Annette is good.*

My mother had lifted up her pride for her children as if she had been hanging clothes on the line, but she also aired our misdeeds to others, mainly as a way to compare one side of the clothesline with the other. I didn't know how to take in that comparison. While she had hoped it served as motivation, the contrasts served to deflate her insecure middle child. Whatever love she gave, I didn't know how to accept it, only how to be good. And that definition changed over time.

I didn't have the long conversations my sisters had with my mother. I didn't have my mother's cooking prowess, and I didn't have her welcoming persona. But what I did have was the knowledge of how to stay in the lines when coloring.

It was a process I had followed. As she abided by her recipe for zucchini pancakes to ensure the desired outcome was crusty on the outside, tender on the inside, I had a desired outcome too.

Attention from my mother.

After college, I grew out of my fuming phase, for which my mother was thankful. And my first marriage helped me become closer to her. I began to see the woman and not the mother, and she began to see the older and kinder me, not the younger bratty one.

Then, in my thirties, with life falling back into its chronological order, our son was born four weeks early, despite my reading *What to Expect When You're Expecting.* My mother had delayed chemotherapy treatments for herself to travel to Oregon after Davis was born. Then my young husband was diagnosed with cancer. She yielded whole weeks of her life to cook and clean and care for my son for the three years Devin survived and many more weeks when I became a single mother.

She had possessed a long, strong record of showing up. "Wherever there is the need," she'd said. And I realized that no matter how much I struggled to *Be Good*, my mother was good without effort, without complaint.

By the time I had turned forty and remarried, my mother was beginning to show signs of dementia. She couldn't write a letter to advise me to *Be Careful, Be Studious,* and *Be Good.*

For months after my father died, my attempts to care for my mother still centered on being good to achieve the desirable result. I was good if I made certain the nurses kept to my mother's bedtime rituals or her medications, or followed up with the podiatrist, or if I made sure her nails were painted, convinced her to attend watercolor craft, or coerced her into playing the game Finish the Phrase by whispering the answer in her ear. If I did the right things, she would see me as *being good.*

I was also trying to make up for my father's death, for anyone who didn't visit because it was hard. It **was** hard. And it took an emotional toll on me and on my reservoir of courage. It took setting aside other aspects of my life. I did it anyhow, because that's how I knew to *Be Good.*

But it wasn't until I gave up on perfection—because there was none to be had in my mother's dementia—that I saw her love for me. And I didn't have to *Be Good* all those years to earn that love. I don't think my mother had ever wanted me to be perfect in my behavior.

Good simply became enough.

Enough, my mother shouted in the middle of Mass, when the chaplain bellowed forth, "The Old Rugged Cross." Or when a mumbling resident had gone on too long about the bird that had flitted away twenty minutes earlier.

Enough, I said, walking out of her care home after my mother yelled at me for reading the newspaper to her. For ten minutes, I sat and sobbed in my car. Later, I relayed the story to my husband and swore I wouldn't go back.

Enough, I saw in my mother's eyes one day when I felt her touch was magic, as if she had waved a wand and filled me with all she had left.

Enough, I felt, no longer needing to read her letters to understand what it meant to Be Good.

Sometimes, All You Can Do Is Show Up

(with Cookies)

THE ULTIMATE
PIZZELLE MAKER

In which I try to match the crispness of my mother's cookies.

I glanced down at my mother's slanted handwriting on the pages of her homemade cookbook. Tears stung my eyes and their salt stung my lips.

My mother was still alive but she no longer wrote anything despite my efforts to put a pen in her hand during arts and crafts, or have her sign her name to a birthday card for her granddaughter. Maybe she had forgotten how to write, or maybe she was just tired after years of rolling and cutting and scooping and mixing. My mother's handwriting was beautiful, neat, yet her grade school teacher had warned she gripped the pen too tight and someday she wouldn't be able to hold her hand steady.

I flipped through the yellowed pages of that cookbook and read aloud the names of the cookies she had once made: *Biscotti, Torcere Friggerre (Twists), Corn Flake Wreaths, Pecan Cups, Pizzelles.* I wanted to eat something made by hand. Her hands. But mine would have to suffice.

Every holiday season, I dragged out my mother's cookbook from its hiding place in my pantry. I was ashamed that I hadn't cooked or baked my way through her collection of recipes but I opened the book to the most-used page and slid my greasy electric pizzelle maker out of its box. All to recreate Christmas in the same fashion my mother had over those fifty years of mine. As usual, I grew despondent throughout the course of baking because I never matched my mother's holiday prowess. She took to baking like a spinner to wool, to weave comfort for her family and make Christmas out of every cookie cutter, sugar sprinkle, pot of oil and pizzelle iron in existence. Next to God, no one spun Christmas better than my mother.

Early mornings and late nights throughout the Decembers of my childhood, my mother had taken up her post in the basement of our Lincoln Street home, where a second kitchen had been installed mainly for a time of year that filled our house with yeast and yum.

Now, I occupied a similar post, but standing at my kitchen island where I gazed out at the daylight on my bare rose bush. I heaved up my mother's Italian ceramic bowl onto the counter to mix the sticky egg-based dough, keeping in mind my mother's note: *Let the dough rest for a while.* I envisioned her at my side whispering that secret to me.

While waiting for my pizzelle press to heat up and the oil to burn off, I listened for noises in the house. I could almost hear my mother. She would have been in our family's basement where I might have joined her to sprinkle or roll—*not too much, not round enough, slow down.* I heard those echoes as I had said the same thing to Davis when he had been little and helped mix dough that would come close to tasting like my mother's, but never really.

I wasn't a talker, and my mother and I hadn't had access to the Internet's wide variety of information the way my son and I had when we conversed over mostly sports while teaching him to make pizzelles. But I loved being in my mother's presence, watching in awe as her hands poked a fork beneath the tendrils of a fragile pizzelle cookie and lifted it to a cooling rack.

In another life, our family would have packaged my mother's pizzelles. Nowadays, I would never buy the manufactured kind in the grocery stores or restaurants. I found them stiff, overpriced, too perfect. The magic behind homemade pizzelles was the diamond, tear-dropped or floral patterns on the press. No one cookie would roll off the press with the same adornments. There would be no perfection for the woman who craved it— perhaps that's why my mother favored these cookies—or for the woman who craved being like her perfect mother. Perhaps that's why I liked baking those cookies: Whereas I strived for her perfection, she could let go.

Regardless, those manufactured cookies would never have tasted like my mother's, first because there was no snap of anise or crunch of actual fennel seeds inside them. Second, the cast-iron press my mother used— which had to be flipped over a stovetop burner in the time it took to say a Hail Mary (according to the legend of the Italian Nonnas)—was rarely used in commercial ventures. And third, to reproduce the taste profile of my mother's pizzelles, one needed to incorporate not only the smears of real grease but also the years of elbow grease poured into each cookie ever to come off her press.

When the pizzelles were rolled out for public consumption, many mouths watered. When a family friend, like Father Weber, came to visit. When my mother's pinochle club arrived for Christmas cheer. When boyfriends of my sisters passed through the carousel of my father's indifference. When the one girlfriend of my brother stayed. When the grandkids finally arrived and their first cookies were not Zwiebacks bought in stores but biscotti and pizzelles cranked out fresh that day by their grandmother.

Twelve years prior, grease caught on fire in the basement at my parents' home during the making of some Christmas cookie or another, most likely the hint-of-honey twists. The fire department was called. A portion of the linoleum floor and Formica countertop had to be replaced. And still, my mother baked on.

I pressed the last of the rubbery dough into the pizzelle maker and scraped one final swath of dough off the wooden spoon with my teeth. Like my mother, I sometimes made pizzelles with the added sting of fennel seeds, much to my children's consternation. They preferred vanilla with a zest of lemon. Or the chocolate ones, a flavor my mother attempted years later. There was a chill in the house that day, coming through the floorboards of our 150-year-old home. As long as I pressed the cookies during the coldest of winter days, simulating the frigid basement of my youth, they cooled to the right amount of crispness.

I surveyed my collection of snowflake cookies spread out across the cooling racks and sighed. Too many of them had browned edges. The cookies had come close to looking and tasting like my mother's, but not close enough.

Still, the next morning, I wrapped the pizzelles into waxed paper and carried a batch to my mother.

With the same reverence my mother had displayed when she put forward her platter of holiday cookies for guests, I kneeled down in front of her while she craned her neck to watch *The Golden Girls* on television. I presented the pizzelles to her as if she were queen of the baking court and

I was waiting for her to knight me.

My mother grabbed one pizzelle and the next and held them high, like an offering of communion. "Oh these," she said a few times through chewing. Crumbs stuck to her lips, cracked from winter's dryness.

She grabbed another and ran her fingers along the creases. "Oooooh, theeeese!" Though stiff, her hands knew how to delicately hold the remembrance. She beamed and I salivated, witnessing as the buttery pizzelles melted on her tongue, slid down her throat and filled her belly, if not her mind, with memory.

In that moment, I loved my mother's cookies because they satisfied a need, but I loved her a little bit more.

MAKING CHRISTMAS
NOT SO BLUE

In which
my mother tells
Elvis to shut up.

"Hey, you, come here. Come here," my mother called out to the man dressed as Elvis who was busy singing "Here Comes Santa Claus" to an audience that had forgotten the names of both Santa Claus and Elvis, but still loved music and presents.

I recalled those days when I had dragged myself to my son's Christmas concert. The one that lasted all of an hour, maybe even half? And I had hoped and prayed my kid would do what he was supposed to do in his "starring" role.

As caregiver to my mother, those challenging days were back.

The impersonator was giving a special performance of Elvis' songs from his Christmas album released in 1957, when my mother would have known and perhaps derided his style because of her devotion to Sinatra. Maybe that's why she shouted at the singer, "Would you just shut up?" I twisted around in my chair, looking for Becky, the activities director. Together, we laughed off my mother's demands.

While I admired the many caregivers and nurses who cared for my mother, the most difficult, yet rewarding role in her care home was that of an activities director. How should one plan for events with a demographic that lost their concentration easily, ate snacks and forgot they had eaten them, but also possessed an adult orientation and wisdom and set of experiences in life?

Recently, a friend had reached out to meet for coffee. She wanted to talk about her mother who also experienced dementia. And moves—how many were too many? I had plenty of expertise.

Over her steaming mug, my friend had said she wanted to move her mother—again. "That would make three moves. How do you know if you're picking the right one?" she asked, stirring more sugar into her cappuccino.

After the course of my mother's four moves, not all of which I was proud of, I had perfected my response. *You could only know if it was the right one for right now.* Coffee roiled in my stomach. The topic brought up so many memories of decisions I should have made earlier. And regrets for the ones I had made too late.

But that's not all I had told my friend. I'd also struck upon a different thought after having spent time at my mother's care home during two separate Christmas events. I had long been a proponent of assessing the culture and feel within a care community. I called it a vibe, but there were certain pieces of information I gleaned through my powers of observation—and immersion. I dropped my spoon, blew on my coffee and said, "Meet the activities director." She looked at me with surprise.

While my mother was still able to engage (**express herself** and **cuss** are two other terms I would also use interchangeably), I wanted to ensure she had the chance to interact with whatever guests came into her life on any given day, whether that person was an Elvis impersonator, a chaplain or women from the local church who came to pray the rosary—only to have my mother throw her beads at them.

But it wasn't just the guest appearances on the calendar that were important. Plenty of centers could program a calendar full of events. But were they meaningful opportunities and did they make my mother feel at home? More importantly, who was actually behind the programming? Who was responsible for knowing how to coax my mother while I was absent and knew where she was in any moment of the day, mentally and sometimes physically, and what activities she would deem interesting enough—for a time—to keep her away from the door (and not set off the alarm) when the temperature fell below freezing outside? Who would get the residents to come to events even if the residents showed no interest at first? My mother always said *No* until someone coaxed her.

My mother was yelling at Elvis. "Who's going to bring your baby back?"

I tried to quiet her down, but I had failed at that since my birth. "Hey,

Mom. That's Elvis," I said and patted her on the knee. "With his blue suede shoes? He's quite the hunk a burnin' love, isn't he? He's pretty good, right? Sounds just like him."

The singer paused.

"Good. Yes. He's large though," my mother said with her eyes wide open staring at Elvis' round belly. A few staff members took in a collective gasp.

"Yes, Mom. Elvis did get quite large. But he was maybe about 150 pounds at the height of his fame." His weight at the time of his death was closer to 350, but she didn't need more details to pile on her criticism of the chubby impersonator.

She nodded, though still fixated on the hefty Elvis in front of her, pointing to him several times.

He went right on and sang "Santa Claus is Back in Town," nearly daring my mother to interrupt him again.

For me, holiday events were designed as an opportunity to witness how all the staff interacted with my mother and other residents. Would they dance with the woman who always quoted Telly Savalas? Events were a chance to witness how the other families also engaged with residents. Did the couple that knew Miss Kathy from church sing with Miss Helen because they knew she loved her music? In essence, how well did other families know my mother and the other residents?

If the activities calendar was plentiful, there was also a chance for me to take a break from being the person who oversaw care of my mother and just be me, a person she might recall.

Like I did at all Christmas shows, I ate too many cookies and cried one too many times at Elvis' versions of "White Christmas" and "Silent Night," though my mother would have preferred some Sinatra song beckoning her children to come home.

The holidays were especially difficult for those like me with a mother in a care home, mourning her life left behind, a life I couldn't recreate. Memories of the past often overtook the fleeting joy I felt in the present.

But those programmed events also served to remind me that, when I was little, my mother had sat through countless practices and performances of my portrayal of the Little Drummer Boy in third grade. She had listened as I'd whined and pulled on the too-tight white leotards, or complained about wearing a short, red tunic, akin to a dress. She and my father drove into downtown Cleveland three nights in a row while I performed before a live television audience and, the next day, she called all her friends to tell them to watch when it aired later on the local public station.

Now, it was my turn to listen to my mother protest about not getting her cookies right away. "Hey! Hey, how 'bout over here?" She snapped her hand to draw the attention of the woman with the plate of red and green frosted cookies.

Or, because the music was too loud and the lyrics sounded garbled to her, she scolded Elvis, "Oh, would you just hush already."

My mother had pressed and boxed that drummer boy tunic of mine and gifted it to me years later as a testimony to her patience. Now, holiday events were a test of my patience and the activities director was there to make certain I passed.

THE SACRAMENT
OF COOKIES

In which
I give more.

The tradition began on a Friday. I was rushing, with plans to leave the city for the weekend and made a quick stop at Busken Bakery close to where my mother resided.

"I'll have a cream-filled Long John," I said to the clerk and also placed a pound of pre-boxed tea cookies on the counter.

The donut was for my grumbling stomach. The tea cookies, buttery rounds of deliciousness topped by a dollop of colored icing, were a payoff of sorts for the caregivers to watch over my mother while I was away, but they would come to mean more than just a bribe.

I paced down the halls frantic to find my mother, knowing I still had more work to do at home before leaving. I bumped into Angela, an older caregiver who was folding clothes, and produced the sweet bounty of colorful tea cookies from behind my back.

She squealed, "Yes! I love those. And girl, I'm hungry."

Janice, my mother's regular caregiver, moaned. "I'm trying to lose weight," she said, despite the fact she didn't need to after chasing after the ever-active residents and feeding, clothing and bathing fifteen residents on a daily basis. She should have rewarded herself with a cookie for all that running around.

I found my mother rocking in a chair and watching *Three's Company* reruns. I wondered if she noticed Mr. Roper's sexual innuendos. She didn't laugh during the laugh track. I waved the open box in her sight and her hand reached for a yellow frosted cookie. She grabbed several more cookies and dented the swirled frosting on each.

Miss Betty, a resident with white hair recently styled at the salon, beckoned me toward her. Charming and cunning all in one instant, she said, "Hey, I'll pay you if you bring me in a full box for myself."

Miss Betty and I had made peace over the years. She had once accused my mother of kicking her little dog, Nibbles. She could have been right.

Now I said, "Miss Betty, you don't need to do that. I'll bring them in for ya." I handed the box to her on the proverbial silver platter.

Miss Betty said, "They better be Busken. Those Servatii cookies are Italian and they're not made with the same butter as Busken." Standards were standards even if for someone with memory loss.

But Miss Betty had insulted a whole forest of my Italian, cookie-making family trees. She was wrong in her presumption that Servatii cookies were made by Italians. The bakery was named after a café where the cookies were sold in Münster, Germany. The location was near the Church of St. Servatius, an Italian saint. *And, the cookies were made by Germans.*

However, the rest of the residents had been quite content, even thrilled with my contribution.

I left in a flurry that day and it wasn't until I drove home that I thought about the length of time my mother had lived at her care home. Four years. Four years of evaluating my relationship to my mother's disease. Four years that offered me the gift of loving and caring for her. Four years that I hadn't quite recognized my mother and the other fourteen residents on her corridor needed more from the outside world than family members, entertainers, and religious figures to bring them joy.

They needed the sacrament of cookies.

Astounded to see how much the other residents down my mother's corridor loved the cookies, I continued to bring a box of cookies for them and the staff. Always on a Friday based on my location in that part of town. But not every week.

A full year passed before I added *Cookies for Arden* as a Friday entry in my mobile calendar and routinely began fulfilling my duties, but without the added donut for myself—my mother's waistline had earned it and mine had not.

My mother once had fulfilled a similar duty on a September day in 1994, for my first marriage to Devin. She baked my favorite varieties of her

Italian cookies, pizzelles, rolled Italian cookies, nut rolls and nut horns. She lined them up in old May Company shirt boxes layered with waxed paper and transported the goods from northern Ohio to Cincinnati in the back of my father's Suburban.

My entire family of seven carried the cookies across Fountain Square through Oktoberfest Zinzinnati and spilled beer, holding the boxes over our heads, to our wedding reception at the Banker's Club, thirty stories above.

No image better signified my mother's dedication to cookies as consecration than that of white department store boxes filled with cookies, bouncing along the heads of siblings who were bouncing to the German oompah beats, toward the cookies' eventual consumption that night.

For over a year, wherever I was in the world, at home with the dog, teaching a writing class, in Oregon or northern Ohio, if it was Friday, *Cookies for Arden* popped up on my phone screen and my stomach ached for the goodness of the cookies and the grace of the women on my mother's hall.

One Friday, the reminder flickered again on my screen. "Yes, yes," I spoke out loud to the phone. "I got it."

An hour after my shower, I stopped by Busken Bakery.

The bakery cases were vacant, as if the cookies had packed up and left town for vacation. "Where are all the tea cookies, where are the sprinkled ones?" My heart pounded. I couldn't show up empty-handed.

The clerk offered a morsel of relief. "Oh don't worry. They're in the back. We got wiped out today. It was back to school week."

"Phew!"

In a matter of minutes, she loaded up a box with piles of red, blue, green and white and sprinkled mounds of buttery cookies while I wondered who got to pick the color themes and schemes that topped the cookies week to week. That was a job for which I would be better suited than caregiver.

I stepped through the doors of my mother's place and the receptionist immediately spotted the gold-foiled box with a plastic window into the world of delight. "It must be Friday."

I lifted up the box with a broad grin on my face. "You bet."

As I entered the kitchen of my mother's hallway, many of the women sat around their breakfast table.

"Hello, girls," I said. I always called them girls or said, "Hello, ladies," because I liked the sound of it. "I've got cookies." I shook the box and gold gleamed in the morning haze of dust particles.

Miss Janie's face lit up at the word *cookie*. Her eyes said, "Yes," even if she couldn't reach for one herself.

Miss Reneta was relegated to a corner table filled with wooden abacus-like toys. She picked out a green one, opened her mouth and mumbled, "Thank you," and her visage returned to a blank stare.

Miss Betty proposed payment, again, for the entire collection. I politely declined. "Can I have three?" she asked. I wouldn't deny her, though she alone remembered the secret hiding place where the cookies were stored.

While Miss Betty picked out her favorites, my eyes fell on my mother's face, turned toward the sun's rays waving back at her. I breathed in that image, one of serenity. Suddenly, her hands fluttered in the air and she snapped her fingers. "Hey, hey." She finally acknowledged my presence—and the cookies.

I inched toward her, and bowing, bestowed upon her the open box resplendent with rainbows of cookies. She fingered three of them, placed a blue one wholly in her mouth, and clasped another blue cookie and one with sprinkles, crushing the swirl of icing between her fingers.

I decided not to eat a cookie. I didn't want to take away from their gift. Besides, the women, with their delight, were the ones actually giving me a gift instead.

I stashed the box on top of the microwave where the staffers knew to look for the prize. The hiding place was like the cookie drawer in our home on Lincoln Street though my mother never stored her **good** cookies there—only the Keebler packaged ones. The good cookies were kept locked away in old Charles Chips cans.

At the last minute, I turned around, reached back toward the microwave and swiped a cookie for myself.

It wasn't a ceremony or a tradition—I decided that day—if I didn't join the residents whom I had grown to love. It wasn't a home if we didn't all share in the heartache and heartburn and calorie consumption. And it wasn't a community if we didn't experience the blessings of one another.

UNINTENDED
CONSEQUENCES OF CARING

In which
families pitch in
to help each other.

With narrowed eyes and a pointed nose, Rita plunked forward from behind her walker. She caught me in her sight as I arrived to see my mother, halted, and asked a question in her gravelly voice. "Miss, excuse me. Miss, do you know what time it is?"

Before I could break into a song by the group Chicago, Rita raised a second question, her eyes peering over glasses. "Miss, excuse me. Miss, can I make a phone call?"

Conveniently, Rita had seven children. When it came time to care for her in her old age, it was good to have the same number of children as there were days in the week. They took turns each day stopping by and she set her clock by the times when her children came to visit. If they did not arrive according to Rita's expectations, she asked for the phone to find out why.

Reaching out with those questions, Rita confused me for someone who worked there, someone who could help. I tried. "It's one o'clock," I answered to the first question.

A caregiver laughed heartily and stepped in to get the next one. "Miss Rita, one of your children will be coming soon." Four o'clock, or three, or maybe not until five the next day, because one child had already visited. But always, each day.

Rita glanced up at the round wall clock in the kitchen, ticking the minutes away.

When I'd moved my mother into her care home, I'd felt the weight of my father's death. I rarely paid attention to the comings and goings of other residents. Who was new? Who was only short-term care while a loved one attended to other business? I didn't consider the challenges or playfulness of the staff. Which caregiver was pregnant? Which one was getting married?

Over the years, residents had transitioned from their place in the hallway asking for the phone or the time to a place in my heart. And when residents died, those who remained—the family of loved ones, caregivers, other residents, and me—shared in our grief.

A month later, Rita was dead. She had lived at the care home for the four years my mother had resided there. She had become like family to all the residents. Rita's family was like family to other residents and caregivers. It was how this place worked. It was why this place worked. It was a closely-held secret only because one had to be on the inside to experience it. Families and caregivers shared laughs and cries, driving tips and restaurant ideas. We pitched in to help each other.

I hugged plenty of residents when I was around, feeling joyful or in need of hugs myself. Many guests hugged my mother when I was absent or away. At present, my mother was keen on a visitor named Mike and his soothing voice, while white-bearded Mike chatted with and spoon-fed a wife experiencing younger-onset Alzheimer's. His wife murmured and her eyes, framed by blunt cut bangs, lit up at her husband's presence but she didn't chat much back. My mother didn't care about interrupting them. Mike didn't either.

In Rita's dying days, her large family had filed in and out of her room and mourned the passing of time. Those of us with loved ones in residence knew to let them alone. Families also knew to manage on their own, so the staff could offer support to Rita's family when necessary. If my mother had a need, such as finding a lost slipper, I could certainly take on that task so caregivers could be available to Rita and her family. Stay close to the grief, but not in it.

When Rita passed away, I observed several of the caregivers in their loss. There were usually two or three dedicated ones to each corridor, based on daytime and nighttime shifts and staffing levels. They had grown to be like family to Rita's large family. Most did not attend the funeral to grieve. Long lost relatives, high school friends, townsfolk, and priests who appeared at Rita's service would never know the round, freckled, concerned or smiling faces and deft, skilled hands and carpel-tunneled, elastic-bandaged wrists of those who had touched their loved one.

Where did the caregivers go to grieve?

No one called them to carry the casket. No one sent them sympathy cards or flowers or picture collages. No one asked what the deceased should wear, the navy blue wool cardigan or the soft, sparkling red one (go with soft), or how she had her hair styled by the stylist or how the barber who had faithfully served him cut his hair through many months of hardship and forgetfulness. The staff and caregivers knew those facts better than any family member.

The caregivers weren't left behind with fond memories of Rita when she had been a striking twenty-something, a middle-aged mother or a sixty-year-old grandmother. They only had recollection of a woman who had grappled with life in a most vulnerable state. They did the greatest amount of work and worry at the most critical period of time.

I slowed when I passed Rita's room. An angel printed on a sheet of paper hung on her door to let all know she had left us. She was gone, her family of seven too, and caregivers paused at the entrance to her room or walked with a little less lightness in their steps as they passed it. The length of time Rita had spent in the care home, the family's unwavering commitment to their mother and other residents such as Betty—whose nails Rita's daughters had painted—and the caregivers' dedication, meant Rita's death left a hole in that little universe of life, alien to so many on the outside of those walls. Her room's photographs of multitudes of toothy grandchildren and the nameplate my mother read like a kindergartener were removed and I felt a void in the erasure of her presence and wished they could have left her room intact forever.

The day I learned Rita died, I sought out my mother and squeezed her a little tighter, to which she yelled back. I embraced the female residents and some of the men a little longer. When the residents giggled at me, nestled into my shoulder, high-fived me for a Xavier basketball win or grasped my hand as if holding on the handlebar of a bike, I wanted them to stay with me, there in that place, longer.

Rita's two questions echoed through the corridors and I tried to answer them without her in my sights.

"Miss, do you know what time it is?"

Yes, Miss Rita. It's almost four o'clock. Time for one of your children to be here.

"Miss, can I make a phone call?"

You don't need to make a phone call. You've reached us through our hearts.

EATING SOAP

In which
I learn
not to lie.

"Young lady, if you're lying to me, I'll wash your mouth out with soap," my mother once said.

I was twelve. I had sworn on the Holy Bible but that wasn't enough evidence to convince her I was telling the truth about my whereabouts after a nine p.m. curfew.

Did she plan to use Ivory or Dial? Or would she choose Saddle soap, which no self-respecting shoe store family went without? Her options also included the dreaded Fels-Naptha soap, which I had used a fair share of in my short life to fight off the unrelenting itch of poison ivy.

"I'm not lying," I'd said, my face hot and wet with tears. Really, I wasn't...that time.

Regardless, my mouth had received a hardy cleansing—with her choice. Ivory.

Now, my eighty-eight-year-old mother lay in a hospital bed in the emergency room.

Only twenty minutes had passed since the night nurse from my mother's memory care home had phoned me. "Your mom swallowed or took a bite out of a bar of soap. Her face is swelling from some sort of reaction. I called the ambulance."

She had eaten soap?

Seeing my mother in bed hooked up to IVs and a heart monitor, I cringed at the fear and rage swimming in her eyes. "Oh, Mom." I shivered as she stared at me with a look of terror in her eyes. My presence in a strange environment caused confusion and an anxiety she could not articulate. "It's okay. It'll be okay," I said, sounding a lot like her. I ran my sweaty hands along her arm.

She tried to speak, but nothing audible came out.

From the other side of the bed, the diminutive doctor said, "Say, ahhh," and my mother opened her jaw while he tapped a tongue depressor around the sides of her mouth.

I peered over the bedrail and saw bubbles forming on the back of her tongue. Her breath smelled fragrant. Like lotion.

My mother shook her head and refused to open any wider so the doctor turned to me and asked, "Do you think she would let you put your fingers in her mouth and root around, see if you can get pieces of the soap out?"

What?

I didn't want to make my mother angrier than she already was but we were running out of time and the swelling continued. I snapped on surgical gloves and poked around in her mouth, clearing out a few slippery white bits that, yes, resembled soap.

Then she bit down on my finger. Hard.

"Ow," I said and pulled my hand out.

The doctor returned to examining my mother's neck. "How did they find her? Is she on any new meds? What kind of soap? Where did she get it? Are you sure it's soap?"

What was it about soap that caused some people to doubt the veracity of others?

"Hotel or designer variety," I answered. I didn't understand why we were having this conversation given the severity of my mother's condition. "I guess she found the soap in someone else's room, probably brought in as a present by a visitor. They found her in the same person's room during their quarter hour checks. No, the staff is really good at keeping out stuff that the residents might ingest without knowing what it is. No, no new meds."

One youngish medical resident remained adamant while typing on a keyboard, not paying attention to my mother or me. "Soap wouldn't do this." Soap, he meant, wouldn't be responsible for such a severe reaction that my mother would not respond to the standard medical protocol of Benadryl or steroids. I wasn't sure either.

But a few years back, my mother had eaten Styrofoam Easter eggs from an artificial flower basket and her lips had puffed up. She was known to gnaw at whole onions and chew on an entire wheel of cheddar. I said, "No, it's soap. The nurse kept the bar. There are teeth marks on it."

Infuriated by the young doctor's disbelief, I repeated the story to the ENT, the pharmacist, the nurses and residents in the ICU, over the phone to caregivers at Arden Courts and to family and friends.

I needed comic relief from what could become a life-threatening situation for my mother. While the doctors determined their next steps, I texted my circle of writers to let them know I wouldn't be in attendance that night because of my mother's predicament. *"I'm trying really hard not to get in a **lather** about this."* I didn't know how many of my friends had parents who had washed their children's mouths out with soap when they'd lied or used swear words. But I had no reason to lie now. Lying equaled soap.

Nervous about what might come next, I said to the nurse standing by for more orders, "She's had such a potty mouth lately; it was time for her to clean up her act." Janice, my mother's regular caregiver had recently admitted, "Your mom has been cussing a bit more than usual."

I directly attributed my mother's crankiness level to how often she got outside. Spring rains had streamed into downpours, flooding the flowerpots out her window. Her forays outside were curtailed. That caused consternation on her part, and thus led to a few choice words shared—*Oh, God dammit, what do you know?*—if she didn't like the direction her life or feet were taking in that moment.

The ER doctor returned to the room. "We'll have to sedate her," he said. "Then try for a nose probe. Next will come a breathing tube, if we can get that down her throat." It was beginning to sound more like torture than procedures. "If that doesn't work, then we'll do an emergency trach."

I nodded, trying to keep track of the number and the severity of the medical procedures he'd rattled off.

The doctor finished his summation. "Do you understand how severe this is?" he asked with a life or death tone in his voice.

"A **trach**?" I asked.

"A tracheotomy," he said.

Why did doctors always assume the rest of us had the same medical training they did? If they uttered a big word, they should make the assumption I knew nothing at all. I hadn't been thinking about the swelling in the deep layers of skin causing harm, but suddenly I developed an unwanted, but warranted, interest in respiratory care.

A nurse shooed me off in Mom fashion despite my protest to be at my mother's side and endure whatever she did. That was how I coped with the fear of what she had to face, a bullet I couldn't take for her. The nurse instructed me to wait outside the room.

In sandals I had hastily slapped on, I tapped my toes like piano keys and stared at my feet. I needed a pedicure. The heron blue color and my mother's hospital predicament were now chipping away at my hopes for spring. I avoided the sympathetic faces of other patients and staff.

What if. What if the nose probe/intubation didn't work? Any procedure with the word *emergency* in front of it constituted a life-saving measure. My mother possessed a DNR on file, but how would I know where the demarcation line was between helping and harming my mother's life?

I didn't hear any Halloween-like screeches coming from the room. A good sign. The nurse emerged. "The intubation was a success." She nearly put her nose next to mine and squeezed me on the shoulders. I let them fall back into their sockets.

Now, we were encroaching upon forty-eight hours in the ICU, but my mother's breathing tube had stayed put. Her body still didn't respond to the typical treatment of steroids and Benadryl. Her face resembled a puffer fish.

The view of air vents and sewer pipes outside the window made for strange nighttime shadows on the roof and was eerily similar to the jungle of tubes on the inside of my mother's hospital room, lit up like heaven, offering me no comfort. I wept at her bedside. Nurses stood behind me to chart data or hang an IV. Chaplains prayed over my shoulder, handed me rosaries, one for me and one for my mother, and left.

The palliative care team visited but teams were intimidating. I didn't need therapy in that moment.

I needed to breathe more air and my mother did too, so I practiced seated yoga poses. Extended side angle. Forward bend. I undertook more chair yoga that day than most residents who lived alongside my mother practiced in a lifetime. The gravity of the situation was not without consideration. Leave the tube in too long, and there was a greater risk of infection. Remove the tube too soon and leave it up to my mother's devices and the Universe, and then what? Then what?

I recited the DNR instructions, *Comfort care only*, multiple times with an infinite number of doctors, palliative care teams and men and women in collars. I ran through that obstacle course a dozen times in my head. *Comfort care only*. But never in my heart.

She and I, mostly my mother, were on a collision course with the future. And the future might not like what it saw and neither did I.

I had traveled the road of bodily decline with a first husband who had died of cancer. I was keenly aware of the potholes and turnoffs and rest stops and orange signs for detours along the way. But my past experience didn't make the situation easier. In fact, decisions became more complex. As the Health Care Power of Attorney for my husband, we had discussed his wants. As the POA for my mother, siblings were involved. My mother had dementia. When my father was still alive, I would beg him to tell me what he wanted for my mother. He would only answer, "You know, your old man isn't going to live forever." And at no time in the past four to five years had my mother been able to confirm to me what she had first articulated in her living will.

And now, what was her destination other than death or the relentless routine of recovery? Meds. Doctors. Physical Therapists. Eating on her own again. Walking. Walking. Walking. Sleeping. Sitting Outside. Wheelchair? Yes, no, maybe. Soft foods diet? Yes, no, maybe. Return to her care home? Yes, no, maybe. Recognize me? Yes, no, maybe.

There existed the dilemmas not accounted for in the Do Not Resuscitate order on her Power of Attorney for Health Care document. They were the small ones that ate away at the intent of her signature on the form. The big decisions were easy to make, even obvious when the time came. But how many little dilemmas were insignificant if taken separately, and when added together, constituted a violation of my mother's wishes?

A new male face appeared in the doorway to my mother's room. He told me he was a specialist in ear, nose and throat issues. The diminutive man looked upon me with droopy eyes in line with a long face. "There's a new drug we can try. It works for other situations, not really this one. But it's worth a try."

I nodded my head eagerly. "Yes, let's do it."

If it worked, there would be a noticeable difference in her facial swelling within a few hours. And **if** the medication produced measurable results, the doctors would remove the tube and my mother could breathe on her own.

Five more hours of chair yoga and team visits ticked off on the clock. My mother slept off and on. I did not.

Finally, the ENT doctor stepped into the room, trying not to be noticed. He circled his stethoscope around his patient's chest and throat as if he were performing a sonogram searching for life.

On my laptop, I wrote, *Good vibes, good vibes, good vibes.*

He bent over my mother's chest and face. Did he see in her eyes everything she was afraid of—being alone, unable to recall her own name? All that she had lost—the husband, a child at birth, one to alcoholism, others scattered away from home? He stooped over his patient again. Were her eyes more alive and aware than before?

I stopped typing. If the doctor could hear anything, I wanted him to hear the slightest sigh.

A small-boned man with a large responsibility, the doctor whispered, "I heard a gurgle."

My eyes rose to meet his dark brown ones. A hint of sunlight was captured in them.

"A what?"

"A gurgle."

Half expecting the doctor to proclaim he had delivered a healthy baby girl, I asked, "We've got a gurgle?"

A smile took over his face, making it appear round. There was so much joy but there would be much more waiting. Overnight. Early morning. But I had hung in there, and so had my mother.

The lyrics to Sinatra's "As Time Goes By" passed through my ears. My mother's incident had been a clear case of *do or die*. Though I had played so much Sinatra, the walls seemed to cave and the ceiling drop. I had been unable to absorb the lonesomeness in his music, trying to reach a place I wasn't ready for my mother to travel.

But, we got a gurgle.

When my mother was released back to her residence a few days later, Suzanne, the jovial nurse, asked, "Do you still want that soap?" She had been saving the bar in case the doctors wanted a sample to test. The test would have cost thousands of dollars to determine any cause or effect. Totally unnecessary.

Suzanne handed the bar to me, wrapped in a plastic grocery bag.

I removed it and turned the smooth object over in my hand. The bar was of the Motel Six variety—oval shaped and almond oil scented. I sniffed at it and recognized it as the scent that had come out of my mother's mouth in the hospital. I ran my fingers across the jagged indentations. That was a quality bite, as good a mold as necessary for dentures. No wonder the doctors had challenged me.

I started to cry. I hadn't slept in days, overwhelmed by the decisions I had made. I cried, thinking about how close my mother had come to death. Now she could attend speech therapy and regain the use of her throat in order to yell at me again.

I looked at the bar of soap before putting it in my purse and began to laugh. *Oh, Mom*, I thought. *At least when you washed my mouth out with soap for lying, I knew better than to take a bite.*

MY MOTHER HAS A FIGHT WITH THE EASTER BUNNY

In which my mother
goes on a different sort
of Easter egg hunt.

T he Easter Bunny, a male employee at the care home dressed in a costume, was on the hunt for plastic eggs when my mother stepped in front of the large, fuzzy, white animal.

The grooves in her brow grew deeper. She grabbed the bunny's furry paw. "You, you," she yelled. She meant that he was standing in her way, but her command of the English language was diminishing, which meant her mean words were on the rise. She called out, "You stupid thing."

The bunny didn't say a word because his lips were sewn shut.

My mother should have recalled the Easter Bunny never spoke. But, alas, some holiday traditions had not crossed the span of time and neurons. The animal's muteness was unacceptable to my mother. The bunny's desire to travel on a path crossing hers was not acceptable. The bunny's wish to turn and scamper off was also not acceptable.

Sporting a purple blouse, I now turned all purple. My armpits sweat and I couldn't recall if I had put on deodorant that day. There were times I was ashamed to be standing alongside a woman who uttered such horrid statements. She used to chastise me in high school. "You're ashamed of me," she would say when she arrived to cheer for me at any of my track events or music concerts. I protested that I wasn't, but I was. It was a shame that lived beneath the surface of both of us. She always felt it in being ten years older than the parents of my friends. Why was I ashamed of her? Because, unlike the parents of my other friends, she didn't wear blue jeans. Or, my mother stayed at home and perfected her *parmigiana di melanzane* (eggplant parmesan) while other mothers lunched at a club or sold real estate. I never could decide if it was the shame of an anxious child or a shame I had inherited.

I didn't want her to feel my shame now, but her mood swings drove me mad. They were at the top of my most despised moments with her. I didn't hate my mother in that moment. I hated myself because I hadn't, and might not ever, learn how to adjust to her emotional outbursts.

When my mother was cranky or ornery, my first reaction was to diagnose a bladder infection, a common occurrence in individuals experiencing dementia. The infections created moderate to severe changes in her disposition. Thus, when her mood swerved and curved like an Indy racecar driver, my first thought was *UTI*.

True confession? My very first thought was *Mom is dehydrated.* Then, *bladder infection.* And because a UTI left undiagnosed for too long could lead to complications, panic set in. I would track down a nurse, or a caregiver might inform me the staff had already told the nurse. Then, there was the pause for a person who was incontinent. It was not an exciting time. One of the caregivers would take my mother to the toilet and turn on the running water, to encourage her to pee in order to test her urine.

She certainly could have been experiencing an infection that day.

The Easter Bunny tried to extract his paw and my mother's hand flopped a few times when he did so, as if they were doing the wave at a sporting event.

We escaped one incident, but I wondered what lay ahead of us, other than eggs.

The staff had cooked brunch and the burnt smell of grease floated through the hallways. "The bacon is this way, Mom. Just smell." I inhaled the smoky scent. I don't know if it was the smell, the halt in our progress, or relaxing my shoulders that calmed my mother. But she was soothed and amenable.

Despite the bunny's attendance—it was his event after all—the meal passed without another episode between mother and hare. The chocolates and orange juice overflowed and I was forced to maintain strict oversight in my mother's access to both. Confined to a corner near the window because of our tardiness and her desire for light, her eyes darted back and forth as she watched the youngsters anxiously wait for the egg hunt to start.

One little boy patted my mother on the knee. "I'm in second grade," he said and turned to me. "I think I'm taller than you," he added and pointed his finger at my chest. So I stood up. He was right. Though it wasn't difficult to tower over my five-foot frame, he was unusually tall for his grade.

When two seats opened up in the main area, I guided my mother to another table with a clear view of the children circling in and out, shoving at each other, emptying out plastic eggs, and cramming chocolate eggs into their mouths. I grabbed a pair of felt bunny ears and a pair of ladybug antennae, fiddled with each headpiece and placed the ears on my mother's head (sorry, Mom), and the ladybug antennae on my head (sorry, kids).

My mother's lips parted, first in a slight grin, then she opened them in a wide smile, ready to swallow up all the jelly beans and life before her, including me. In the span of an hour, she had gone from rage at the sight of the Easter Bunny to joy at the sight of the children.

I lived and died a thousand lives in between a bad moment of my mother's and a good one, between a broken egg and a whole one. Her voice, at optimal yelling capacity, reminded me of days back in my childhood when she never separated far from her rubber spatula in case discipline was needed.

New faces with new voices flooded the room with sunshine. Families and residents admired the Easter Bunny and praised our felt ears.

Soon, the bunny stopped by our table again and my mother reached out for his paw.

Oh no, I thought, pulling on my imaginary armor to protect the bunny, not my mother.

But he only rubbed at my mother's new ears with his other paw. She did have the better pair, ones more erect with wider openings than the bunny's. Hers would not flop over.

"Hello," she said to the bunny with a grandmotherly voice.

And because I was wearing the extra set of antennae, her voice rang through to my heart.

Celebrating Eastertime with my mother caused me to reflect on the rising and dying and rising again of her to beat another infection or how her yelling could break the magic spell between us at any time.

At the care home, several residents had recently died due to falls or the natural cycle. I thought about the shaky nature of my mother's existence and mine.

We were all one infection or fall away from the precipice, or one flight away from the opening of skies. We were all one moment away from feeling sheer joy or experiencing complete absurdity, from savoring rich chocolates or finding empty Easter eggs.

CHEERING ON LIVES

In which
I learn
about touch.

"Your mom's in the community room," Becky called to me as I walked briskly down the hallway, but she hadn't said why. On my way to find my mother, a few pleasing notes drifted alongside me. But as I closed in on my destination, the voices didn't sound like singers.

They sounded more like cheerleaders.

I was still shaken from the radio reports I'd heard in the car about a mass shooting in Las Vegas. It was way too early in the day for cheerleading, and it felt inappropriate. Didn't they know how hundreds of people had been killed or injured? How could there be such sunniness in the face of unthinkable tragedy?

Standing at the back entrance to the gathering space, I glanced around the room for my mother. At first, my eyes skipped over her because she was squirming in a wheelchair.

Blood pulsed through my ears as they were again struck by the voices of two women with blonde hair crooning and carousing with the crowd of residents who waved around shakers and tambourines to the classic songs from the Forties and Fifties. They were backed by a female pianist and a male guitar player.

What was this show?

A chorus of residents sang "Baby Face" and one woman, Ginny, curled her hand around the side of her mouth as she boomed out in a baritone voice. My mother joined in at the end with "baaaby faaaaace," sung in her upper register, still angelic.

I watched from the back of the room, suddenly spellbound. Like the bouncing ball over the top of old song lyrics on TV, my mother's rounded eyes followed the women bopping around a room cramped with wheelchairs. The performers nudged the restless residents to rise, like cheerleaders on the sidelines of a sporting event rooting for the home team.

Finally, the two female singers and their accompanists stopped to catch their breath.

"Hi, Mom," I said softly in my mother's good right ear. I clasped her wrists and shook the green, plastic maracas she held in her hands. I couldn't tell her to shake them because she wouldn't. And she didn't. She was resolutely still. Calm. Her eyes were fixated on the fresh faces of the women springing from one resident's side to the next.

After a short break, hints of "Me and My Gal" floated around the room as music filled the space again.

I couldn't budge. Like my mother, I was mesmerized by the high-spirited singers and their musical partners, wearing only the thinnest layer of makeup to highlight the joy they exuded and extracted. The two lead singers' faces gleamed while they danced around wearing black tights and purple sleeveless shirts and swinging their arms in rhythm with the residents.

They also wore contagious smiles.

Becky leaned over my shoulder. "The singers are former NFL cheerleaders. They and the two musicians are part of a non-profit that goes around and plays and sings at care communities and they're coming on Mondays for the next few weeks." The founder of the non-profit, Priscilla, was about my age. After her mother had died from Alzheimer's complications, she started Cheering Voices to bring more cheer into the world of those with dementia living in various care settings.

It was working. I could feel the joy. It seeped into my pores.

A chair opened up next to my mother for me to sit.

My mother wiggled around in the oversized transport chair but she didn't appear likely to get up that day. I could observe without concern for her whereabouts. Each time one of the performers patted my mother's arm or passed her by while dancing to "Ain't She Sweet," her hazel eyes grew brighter and the long lines disappeared around her eyelids.

Throughout five or six more songs, the women met my mother's gaze or that of other residents with an intensity I could not convey, as it was difficult to consistently make that kind of connection with anyone living there.

Julie, one of the performers, slowly ran her slender hands along the sleeve of my mother's sunflower-dotted shirt and my mother stroked the singer's glistening cheek in return.

During the next song, Priscilla, the other singer, stood before my mother, holding and waving her hands. Priscilla locked her arms around my mother but spoke to me. A three-way embrace. "I see my mom everywhere," she said, her eyes batting back what I thought were tears.

I nodded. Her work had become about her mother's life. A mantra I understood.

The middle-aged female pianist played a few notes and prodded the audience on toward the next tune, "Shine on, Harvest Moon." She serenaded the residents and the velvety tones of her voice covered the room in warmth.

Seated next to me, Peggy, a petite and ebullient resident, leaped up from her chair, as if to match the crescendo of energy in the room, and sang along to "I Want a Girl (Just Like the Girl that Married Dear Old Dad)."

When the music ended, Peggy tapped on my arm. "Do you want to see the gal that married dear old dad?" Her hands shook. From between two tattered cards carried in her purse, she removed an old-fashioned, airbrushed photo of her mother.

"She's beautiful. She looks just like you," Julie said.

Peggy beamed. "Everyone says that."

I bent over the photo. "What was your mother's name?"

"Margaret. Just like me." Her chubby cheeks grew round.

I spent whole seconds envious of residents like Peggy who, out loud, had connected the notes of the bouncing ball to the music of their lives.

Like the singers, I, too, saw my mother in everyone. Saw everything she once could do. Speak of her own life, her parents, my father, or me. Dance in the basement as her records spun on a stereo, her body swaying. Though sometimes she moved to a rhythm the rest of us couldn't hear, she couldn't jump up like Peggy to claim those memories.

And my mother was not one to follow directions, so she wouldn't shake a tambourine if I told her to do it.

However, I sensed, from her smile, that she found the presence of the cheerleaders a light in the tunnel of her sometimes-darkened mind. They had found a way inside her with their exuberant voices, a hop in their steps, glowing smiles and compassionate taps on the arm.

Earlier, while sitting in the parking lot with hands glued to my steering wheel, I had debated whether or not to listen to the President's press conference about the Las Vegas shooting. But I had turned off the ignition to clamp down my heart and prevent the flow of heartache from flooding my mother's home.

When I departed ninety minutes later, I faced the bleakness again, this time with more strength.

I had given up cheerleading in ninth grade to try out for volleyball. It was a win-win for many. Throughout that morning's performance, I had shifted my thoughts away from the Las Vegas tragedy back toward my junior high cheerleading days: Stuck grabbing a basketball net while another cheerleader walked out from beneath me. Our seventh grade history teacher had tried to help me down, but I'd dropped to the floor instead. I remembered my cheerleading skirts flipped up by the boys seated behind me in Spanish class. Even worse, I recalled I could never do the splits, not all the way. For me, cheerleading had represented embarrassment and failure.

Until now.

The women had not only rooted for my mother and the others to find a way back to the weightlessness of their younger days but, unknowingly, they had applauded their audience's ever-so-small moments and movements in the midst of a horrific maelstrom that had occurred two-thousand miles away.

Back in my car, as I pressed the ignition button, the memory of the glow that circled my mother's face lit up the interior of my car. In that same music, I had dropped my defenses and allowed myself to be touched.

I imitated one of the cheerleaders and tried to sing with her velvet tones, "I'll Be Loving You, Always," but my voice splintered, thinking about Las Vegas and the victims. And about the need to be touched by music and by hand during the bleakest times in our lives.

Or always.

STILL LIFE WITH JACK

In which
I get to keep
the life Jack lived.

"What, what, what?" my mother asked, distraught as landscapers blew a mess of mulch over the sidewalk and some of the dirt flew across our feet as we strolled. Then she growled at the young men, and marched straight for a wooden bench in the sun where she sat down.

Behind us, Jack wheeled outside. Jack, a younger resident afflicted with Parkinson's, peered into my mother's face. "Hi, Jean," he said.

My mother ignored Jack.

Jack turned to me, pushed a few strands of hair from his eyes, and said, "And I c-can't remember you, but y-you're that g-girl."

I was that girl, that daughter.

We were outside of the care home under a Virgin Mary blue sky with the breeze murmuring in our ears. Jack and I filled the minutes with talk about what constituted the perfect summer day and how to be on the lookout for sunburn.

"M-my mother," he said, "was on a b-boat one time for e-eight, eight hours. She just s-stayed out all day and n-never once thought she needed s-sunscreen." He laughed at his reminiscence. Only later, he said, she had screeched at the mere touch of her arm.

Maybe my mother's presence had unearthed something inside of Jack as she sat, silent though joyful in her surroundings, gold streams of light reflected back in her face. It was the first time Jack had spoken about his mother to me. In the past, we had only talked about his son or his brother and sister.

In the middle of our conversation, Jack's wheelchair rolled back into a bed of irises, crushing the stems, and his tires got stuck. He asked, "P-please?" and for a moment, I saw his life as immobile, caught between concrete and green, between *unable* and *can*. I jacked up the back wheels and heaved him and the wheelchair out of the flowerbed.

The back door opened. "Hey guys," Becky said. "How's it goin' today?" She always spoke in a relaxed voice and I wondered if she was that calm with her young daughter at home.

Of course she had just missed how it was going.

She held in her hand two sets of earphones and iPod Shuffles for Jack and my mother, part of the Music and Memory program I had encouraged her to start up. My mother's playlist was stuffed full of Sinatra while Jack's was populated by Simon and Garfunkel, and there the age difference was apparent.

Becky handed the headsets and music players to Jack and my mother, and went on her way with more to deliver.

I quickly connected my mother's headphones to her iPod Shuffle. I let her mind spin and she beamed at the songs coming through across the wires, messages from long ago, while Jack pushed and pressed at the buttons of his iPod Shuffle.

"Let me try." I held out my hands. I hated to watch him struggle.

"It's n-not w-working," he said and tossed the earphones in his lap. He didn't ask for help.

I had a sense he was not complaining about their malfunction, preferring to continue our conversation. "I u-used to take p-pictures all over the m-marshes in the Carolinas, t-trying to c-capture things m-moving." With his words, he painted for me a vision of sun-tinged reeds swaying in the estuaries where herons played. "N-now, I only t-take s-still lifes."

While Jack stumbled over his words, I wanted to jump in and finish his sentences, despite knowing that was wrong, and also frustrating for him. Numerous times, I bit my lip, held my breath and waited for just the right word to come from his mouth and not mine. But soon, no more came.

In the silence, I studied his face, the ruddy grooves, the graying beard that contrasted with his bright eyes. There was a broad divide between the still life of his photographs as he explained them and the outer life he was leading. He was always on the move. His wheelchair never met a door he couldn't shove open. It was rare for him to be this quiet. Usually he would stop any resident or visitor in the hallway to make conversation. His life was anything but stationary, yet there was a quiet in his mind that I could only suspect, never detect.

"I'll have to see your pictures sometime," I said. It was true. I never lied to any of the residents, unless I was going along with one of their own fabrications. I wanted to see his photos.

"My b-bro-ther has my c-camera. I want my old one b-back. Not this P-polaroid he gave me." He yanked a retro version of a Polaroid camera out of his pocket and held it up. His hands were trembling. "H-hardly works," he said.

I thought it was a clever gift. A niece of mine owned one. Easy to use. Easy to lose. Yet I could see how hard it must have been for him, no longer able to hold a professional camera in his shaky hands.

The sun's intensity bore down on my legs and my mother's, but the rest of our bodies were now shaded. My mother fell asleep and Jack rolled in closer to the coolness.

"D-do you have p-pictures of your m-mother, you know, when she was y-younger?"

She woke up as if on cue, but with the music still playing in her ears, she was living somewhere else, not in the present.

I looked longingly at my mother and images of her as a thirty-year-old tourist in New York City then as a forty-year-old wife leaning on my father's shoulder flashed through my head. "Some," I laughed. "I have some." Actually, I had scores at home, as keeper of many family files, scattered around my office, and stuffed in boxes like a recent one found with my proud mother and a bouncy baby, my older sister, Laura, now in a nursing home following a stroke. Images of my mother were everywhere, stored in my poems, on my hard disk and in my head.

Especially, my mind went to a single photograph of my mother she had proudly displayed for years at her house in a pink photo frame purchased by my sister Jeanne that read M-O-M. The photo showed my mother seated with her four daughters against the backdrop of Rome's Trevi fountain, designed as an homage to the four forces of the sea, like the four forces of her daughters. Of course I understood how Jack felt about photographs and thought I might start to cry.

I fanned my face. "Wow, it's hot, Jack. We need to get back inside." I leaped up.

Jack pushed off with his toes and his chair rolled back into the smashed irises again. I heaved him forward once more and returned him to level ground, then lifted my mother from her seat and escorted both of them inside.

The resident tabby cat was slinking around the activities room as we entered. My mother would never have allowed a cat in her own home but, like the other residents, she was enamored with its slick movements. I said my goodbyes to her and left her in the company of the scampering cat.

Jack wheeled behind me and I tried to part ways with him.

"Can-can you stay more? I have s-something I wanted to s-show you."

I turned to face him. His eyes were as deep blue and mesmerizing as the ocean he had once photographed. "I'm running late for a meeting. But I promise I'll track you down next time."

He was determined to see me to the exit door. The one that separated him from the world. "W-when you come b-back, I'll s-show you some of th-those photographs."

I dropped my head in shame. I only had one heart and that one belonged to my mother. I didn't know how to enlarge mine. But Jack did.

"Do you know why I take ph-ph-otographs of all those marshes and coasts and the water?" he asked, using the present tense to let me know he was still engaged.

I punched in the code to leave before my heart burst, but stopped.

I knew why I took photographs. Why my current count of pictures of my mother was over three hundred in five years' time. Why I captured *morning finds*—odd views that I stumbled across during my long walks in the city that I photographed and posted to social media. Why I took pictures of discarded shoes wherever I found them in the city, or the world. I knew why anyone took pictures. To capture what might be lost.

I thought I knew Jack's answer but wasn't prepared for his response.

"Because I g-get to k-keep the life I lived." He looked relieved once those words were out of his mouth, as if he had held this secret all his life, or at least his life with Parkinson's.

Later, as I unlocked my car door, I had a vision of Jack seated on a small, rugged fishing boat with his camera in hand. Against a backdrop of blue and gold skies, the boat drifted past stems of green rising out of the marshes and floated along the breeze.

THE MYSTERY
OF THE ORANGE FINGERS

In which I am
surprised by my mother's
new obsession.

"Here, Jean the Bean. You can have these to stay busy," Angela said. My mother was seated in a swivel chair at the hair salon in her care home. Angela, an older caregiver, handed my mother an opened bag of Cheetos.

I pursed my lips. My mother was a pretzel eater. I had cleaned out shelves of cream-colored Charles Chips pretzel cans in the family home to prove it. She never ate Cheetos. Never bought Cheetos. Never looked sideways at a bag of Cheetos.

She snatched the bag from Angela's hands, plucked a fat Cheeto from the crinkled bag and rammed it in her mouth.

Apparently, I was wrong.

For close to two hours, I had been visiting with my mother, following a meeting with the executive director for my mother's annual checkup. Her care home—I mean, my mother—passed with flying colors. Afterwards, she led me outside toward plastic lounge chairs still dripping with drops from the morning's deluge, which was right where she sat. In the wet. "Ewww," she screamed but didn't plan to move.

So we sat and listened to insects she claimed she couldn't hear, and counted the different species of trees in our view. We counted six, though she fell asleep a few times with her head on my shoulder during the counting. I melted into her form.

After a time, we wandered back and I led my mother to her hair appointment. That was when Angela handed her the Cheetos.

Now my mother was settled in the vinyl salon chair and I attempted to depart once more. "Mom, you seem a little busy, so I'll just see you later." I nodded at Carol, the hairdresser, hoping she would join in the chorus.

A muffled munching sound came from my mother's orange-rimmed lips.

"You're not going to stay?" Carol clearly wanted me to remain.

If I stayed, then I had to calm my mother or listen as she squirmed and complained, *Oh, that's cold. No, don't do that.* I didn't want to hear my mother argue as Carol snipped away a few millimeters of her lily-white hair.

I thought Carol and I had previously come to an understanding. But we hadn't.

"Sure. I'll stay." My shoulders fell and I sank into the chair beneath the bubbled hair dryer switched to "off."

I prepared for my mother to deliver one of her glares or shout out loud when she didn't like what was happening. Instead, she devoured the Cheetos. Cheetos! Crunchy orange tubes of nothingness she would have never bought at the grocery store. They didn't even taste like real cheese, nutty, floral or otherwise.

Everyone who passed by disregarded my mother's hair. Instead, they commented on the Cheetos in her hands and in her mouth as she sifted through the last of the neon orange crumbs and licked her fingers. My mother smiled back with lips now smeared with a color of orange L'Oréal had yet to invent.

"Oh, they all love Cheetos," the nurse supervisor chuckled, her red hair bouncing as she laughed.

I pictured my mother sneaking up behind unsuspecting residents as Chester Cheetah might do, deftly lifting Cheetos from their bags of snacks. "I'm shocked my mother likes them."

"Your mom eats them all the time," the activities director proudly beamed.

Incredible. I learned something new about my mother though it was nothing from her past. I had spent all this time trying to learn more about her history but I was better off trying to learn about her **now**.

Carol finished clipping her hair. "Do you want me to curl it?"

She had razor cut my mother's white and gray hairs in along the back neckline and left her bangs with a little length, softening what could sometimes be a hardened brow.

While Carol still gave perms to many of the female residents, I no longer wanted that for my mother. She now looked the way she had in a photograph I owned of her as a little girl. I saw in her simple hairdo a five-year-old wearing a prim hat, wool pea coat and proper Mary Janes with tight leotards, holding a play purse years before curlers became a part of her vocabulary and nightly ritual. I saw in my mother a return to her youth.

"No, she's tired and she'll just head to nap and wind up with bedhead. Besides, it looks cute like that." I brushed at her bangs and heaved her from her chair while she held a firm grasp on the Cheetos bag.

I breathed a sigh of relief. My mother could relax after the strenuous activity and I could leave and unwind in my safe space of the car.

Still grasping the flattened foil bag, my mother handed it to me. It was then I noticed her nails, which contained bits of orange dust beneath them. But she walked off before I could do anything about them.

Occasionally, I had discovered that her fingertips were discolored in a shade more toward the ochre family and not natural, flesh tones. The nails appeared stained. I suspected her hands had not been scrubbed well, or she had been eating carrots or sweet potatoes with her fingers. I should have asked myself how many different orange side dishes could the cook possibly serve? Two would have been the response.

Finally, I had the answer to the origin of my mother's Day-Glo orange fingers: Cheetos.

It was a classic Mom *gotcha cha* moment.

I mentally made a list of the reasons my mother should be allowed to eat Cheetos:

1. *She liked the snacks because they were crunchy, as her diet had been softened over time and become quiet. She needed noise, the kind that had been generated when raising five kids. I suspected that's why she still yelled a lot. She wanted to hear what she had to say.*
2. *Residents were eating Cheetos all of the time.*
3. *It was never too late to change from pretzels to Cheetos.*
4. *Cheetos just taste good.*

But the real reason had more to do with genes.

"You liked those Cheetos, right Mom?"

With her back to me, my mother asked, "What's that, honey?" She had already set about the task of lining up the legs of a chair with the seam binder between the carpet and linoleum.

I caught up to her and tapped the bag.

"Cheetos."

She glanced down at the foil wrapper and wiped orange flint off her black pants. She said nothing as if waiting for a big reveal.

"Here's a secret, Mom," I whispered in her functioning ear. "I like Cheetos too."

A Pretty Good Team

BABY, YOU'RE A FIREWORK

In which sparks fly between my mother and me.

The pink light of dawn broke through the drapery in my bedroom and I nudged my husband awake. "I'm taking Mom on a picnic today." Mark wiped his eyes and blinked at the clock. "It's only six a.m."

"Yes, but it's the Fourth of July and I'll need your help."

My mother was always star struck whenever Mark, and his playful, blue eyes, was in her sights. More so than me, he had allowed my mother to be who she was in her disease. He mumbled something agreeable and rolled over while our fluffy dog whacked his tail around in his crate.

I jumped out of bed.

I hadn't taken my mother out in a while, since the effort now required two people to move her. During our previous escape to Eden Park, the antics with my mother had resembled an Abbott and Costello routine. Our arms were in a tangle. I held her at the waist while lifting her leg into the seat well. "Ack, ack, what are you doing?" my mother yelled. The park guests and geese were startled to hear her protests. She stared at me with her hazel eyes graying at the edges like the soft hair around her temples, then sternly fought back with her typical line of questioning. *What car? This car? Why way? This way? Which way is this?* I couldn't go through that again.

Now with my husband and our daughter Shannon, I drove my mother to a nearby community park. When I got out of the car, I stretched my arms and breathed in the smell of fresh-cut grass and I wondered if my mother could smell summer too, or remember my father, swearing about his broken-down mower, in that moment.

Mark and I hoisted my mother's feet from the back seat well, swung her body toward the door opening, stood her upright, and inched her forward. We moved her along a cracked asphalt path toward a picnic shelter with a roof drooping along the shady side. We were the only park guests other than a teenager who hugged a bulky picnic basket while waiting for a friend.

"Where are we?" my mother asked as we all inched forward. She abruptly stopped to gaze at the blue in the sky and asked the question again as we approached the shelter. The lineup of picnic tables reminded me of our family's Fourth of July cookouts.

A collective groan from all five children used to rise up from the house whenever my mother had insisted on eating outside no matter the humidity that befell northern Ohio in July. Soon, Aunt Joan arrived with her traditional baked beans. As an adult, I slurped up baked beans, but back then, I hated them. We all did. As my father grilled the sausages, my mother grilled him about his barbecuing techniques, which always resulted in an added charcoal flavor to the meats and additional wait time or do-overs. Soon all of us kids would be excused from a table blanketed in gold-checked cloths and we'd happily run off to play kickball or bocce ball until called.

My mother's picnics had always included an extra card table with a buffet large enough to feed an NFL team. She topped off the spread with traditional angel food cake frosted with a cool, creamy whip—someone always dragged a finger through the cream—and dotted with tart blueberries and sweet strawberries to honor the stars and stripes, and her marriage.

Yes, my parent's wedding anniversary fell on the Fourth of July. Legend had it, my father's family shoe store closed on the holiday, which, according to my Grandpa Januzzi, made the date perfect for a morning marriage ceremony and evening reception. During my youth, I never recognized the Fourth of July as a special day for my parents. Their anniversary was overshadowed by the country's birthday, neighborhood bike parades, never-ending softball games and Italian sausage with fennel seeds and oregano cooked to a crisp.

After all the activities that could possibly be wrung out of a small town had taken place, we would pile into the station wagon and head to George

Daniel Stadium in Lorain or the Amherst football stadium to watch the booming fireworks. But as my parents aged, they chose to honor themselves in a quieter fashion and celebrated by driving the winding road along Lake Erie to buy an ice cream cone at Toft's Ice Cream Parlor. My mother had loved to park near the lake with the car's nose pointed toward the water. Though she couldn't swim, she was soothed by the endless waves of motion that helped separate the sky from the sea.

Back at the park, morning dew sparkled and danced across the tables. Before we sat down to our meager picnic, Shannon wiped the water off the table with disposable wipes from my mother's supplies. The air was now scented with baby powder, no longer fresh-cut grass. I unpacked slices of cucumbers, bags of Bing cherries and chocolate chip cookies, and my mother's cherished peanut butter and jelly sandwich, food she wasn't served at her home as some might have thought it too pedestrian for the amount of money families paid.

"I'll have that," my mother said and singled out the chocolate-chip cookie. A collective giggle coursed through the rest of us.

By habit, she began to pick at whatever food was left on my plate. I often left the more healthy options or previously pitted cherries in her view for just such occasions. She reached over for the other half of my sandwich. "I'll have some of yours," she said, and stuffed the triangle—she had always cut our lunch sandwiches in triangles, so I did that for her—into her mouth.

Without kids screaming on the nearby swings, I filled the space with stories about the Lorain International Festival, typically held during the first week of July as well. Lorain was my mother's hometown and not only was it in proximity to Amherst but became our adopted hometown. We often straddled the two worlds of the newer sections of the small town of Amherst and the ethnic city of Lorain. The festival highlighted the various nationalities that called the city home and also hosted food tents serving ethnic food where my siblings and I ate pierogi, baklava and stromboli, all in the course of an hour. They also hosted a pageant. I told Mark and Shannon how one year, my sister Laura was crowned Italian Princess and soon after, Miss Congeniality.

Mark chewed through a cookie. "How come you didn't enter the contest?"

My husband might have seen me as an Italian princess, but I didn't. "Who wants to compete with Miss Congeniality?" Besides, I didn't look like a princess. I liked my shorts or jeans. Culottes were my saviors so I could look like a girl and still run around with the boys. "Right, Mom?"

My mother nodded along as she ate a second cookie and crushed the pitted last cherry between her teeth. We had fought for years about my hatred for dresses and I always countered she had three other daughters to dress up.

Soon her chin dropped near the edge of the table and her elbows slipped off the glossy wood paint. She was tired.

I couldn't make her anniversary last forever, not longer than an hour. It was time to go.

We reversed course and returned to her care home.

Once she was settled in an armchair with a tufted cushion in a warm corner of the sunroom, I tried to leave. I really did. But my tears kept me rooted and I walked back toward her and crouched down at her side.

My mother and I had been conjoined for five years. Five years without my father. She and I had grown together in the way a married couple grew together—I could finish her sentences by tone and not thought—except I returned to the outside world and she remained in her inner one.

We weren't going out for fireworks that day. The loud noises would have disrupted her state of peace. She burrowed into the seat and the lack of activity and rubbed my arm. Ironically, I was wearing a short tank dress and she embraced the summer day not for its flash of warmth but because she could touch my skin. She slid her fingers up and down my legs, an act which might have appeared odd to an outsider. But my mother was only admiring the olive skin of her youth and touching something she could love.

Her fingertips pressed on my arm and produced goose bumps.

I had learned to love my mother differently than I once had. My mother was alive and her breath lived in me. But there was some inexplicable spark between us that had nothing to do with mothering or daughtering, because neither of us had accomplished much in those roles our last years together, though we hadn't lacked for trying.

I wiggled my fingers from her hold.

But she grasped my tanned arms again.

My husband and daughter stood behind me and waited a long while. I didn't care. My mother and I had shuffled down too many long corridors together for me to rush goodbyes on that day.

I straightened up and cradled her head as she nuzzled her nose into my soft dress and again wove her fingers through mine, creating a basket to cradle our love.

Suddenly, the Fourth of July burst through me, hot sparks heating my skin cooled from the air-conditioned halls, and filled the moment with fireworks neither my mother nor I could see or hear. But we felt them.

Yeah, we felt them.

In which I learn Tipperary is really not a long way.

M y mother was seated in an upright kitchen chair with its wooden legs full of gouges from wheelchair gears and kicking residents. I pulled another chair alongside hers. Her hair was flattened after a shower where the caregiver must have used a lilac soap. She rested her head on my shoulder like a child in want of a good read. We hummed to Irish tunes bouncing through the halls like Celtic dancers.

"It's a long way to Tipperary," I sang aloud.

"Tipperary," my mother said. "What is Tipperary?"

"A land far, far away," I answered. *Like the one I can't always reach with you,* I wanted to add.

I had spent a long day at a caregiving symposium and hadn't planned to visit my mother. Yet, on that day, like many others, surprises emerged. If I arrived at her care home with cookies, expecting gratitude, or if I showed up with photos for her to see, my best laid plans, together with my mother and me, completely melted down. I'd watch my mother's mood, like a Ferrari, move from stillness to growling in ninety seconds.

But in the rare instances when I had no plan, I saw a pinprick of light in our moments together and I might find my mother laughing and joking about playing kickball inside while a cranky resident, once a scientist, screamed out, "Kickball is an outside game."

This was one of those happy times with **no** plans. My mother and I tapped our toes to the music as I flipped through the pages of a worn *Redbook* magazine. When I landed on the "Food" section, pictures of colorful entrees such as Tagliatelle with Peas and Sicilian Pasta caught her eye. She read each headline and I recited the recipe below. She followed my bitten nails down the page. "That sounds too sweet for me," she said, without the realization that the dish was savory. Or she said, "Too salty," with no understanding of a recipe that called for sugar and dates.

I placed the magazine in my mother's lap but she refused to hold it and it landed back in my hands. Instead, she stroked my knees. My legs tingled. It had been a long time since she had touched me tenderly, but then she reached over my legs and fiddled with the magazine pages between her finger and thumb. She ripped one page then the next from its binding, keeping her hands busy. At least they weren't slapping at mine.

"It's just like we're back in Amherst at the hair salon, Mom. We used to tear apart magazines for the recipes, right?" My pantry was filled with half a dozen baby-sized shoeboxes containing recipes my mother had cut out in straight lines from some magazine or the three newspapers our family used to receive or her cookbooks with yellowing three-hole punch pages containing her handwritten recipes.

My mother burst into chuckles. "Yeah." Then she handed the tattered sheets to me—was she expecting me to cook dinner?—and sang, "It's a long long way to Tipperary..."

Together, we finished, "…but my heart's right there."

Her eyes grew wide as she paged through more and more of the meal section in the magazine. She rarely ate dinners that resembled gourmet anymore. That time was over when she had hosted holiday and First Communion feasts of Italian delicacies—the kind now called charcuterie or small plates in upscale eateries—spread out across banquet tables that my father carted home from the shoe store. Much of my mother's food was pureed now, which left some wiggle room for cookies. She never had problems digesting sweets.

After leafing through the "Food" section and discussing our likes and dislikes for each dish, my mother laid her head on my shoulder again, as if she had consumed an entire meal and now was ready to sleep.

Late afternoon was my mother's naptime. Valerie, her evening shift caregiver once told me, "If I lay her down a little before dinner, then she gets through the meal and has a nice, comfortable evening."

Sleep came on like a train engine, full-steam for her. I let her fall into dreams while my mind followed its own tracks back to the speaker at the caregiver symposium I had attended earlier that day. I was not a fan of conferences because of being caged inside large rooms with no natural light and fed pre-packaged, boxed food. But I did want to hear the featured guest.

John O'Leary, author of *On Fire*, had stood at the podium and posed a question to the audience: "What about my life had offered the opportunity to care for my loved one? And what blessing could I find in the day when given this opportunity?"

On the back of the conference program, I had scrawled an answer, surprised at my quick response. *To witness the transformation of my mother from an older person with a disease into a human being. Not her actual transformation, but the one I am experiencing with my own heart.*

Crash.

A maintenance cart ran into a wall.

My trance was broken.

My mother fidgeted in her blue sweater and crossed her arms to cradle herself as she woke.

"Mom," I whispered to wake her up fully and pointed at my watch.

"Yes?" she whispered back.

"I have to leave." I kept my voice low, wanting to catch her in that elusive moment between sleep and consciousness the way one wakes a baby and knows it is a gift from God.

"Okay, honey." She took my chin in her hands and kissed me on the lips. Did she get this intimacy? Did she still see me as her baby, though I now saw her as mine?

"Oh, you call everyone *honey* these days."

"Yes, you're right," she said. She broke into a smile where the lines on her face radiated out in concentric circles. She patted my hair, plucking some strands from a hairclip.

My bangs and errant threads of hair fell into my soggy eyes. And this time, she let them alone with no judgment.

And didn't she cry ever? I last remembered her crying during Devin's funeral, or possibly when my father walked me down the aisle to marry Mark. I didn't know if not crying was part of her dementia, the disease allowing for her to let go, or was it her simply letting go? If so, what a gift that had been to release all the worry she had carried **a long way** for so many years.

"Ciao, bella," I said in one final goodbye. She threw me a kiss and I tossed her one back.

My mother's past months had been hellish. Mood swings, medical mishaps. Responding to her whims was like being told to evacuate a hurricane and waiting out the storm in a shelter not of my choosing, and certainly not of hers.

Those first weeks of the year had been busy. But she and I had settled back into our rhythms, though not necessarily as mother-daughter. And not always as caregiver-loved one.

It had been a long way to Tipperary and we had simply become *you and me*.

FIGHT OR SWITCH?

In which
my mother
gets a black eye.

"C'mon, c'mon," my mother said. She grasped my hand and whipped my body in front of her as if she were breaking a horse. A clumsy horse, maybe. I tripped over my running shoes.

"Jean the Bean. I love it when your mamma's feisty," a caregiver said as she walked past my mother and me clogging up the hallway.

Feisty was one word I could use. I had a few more for the woman who now sported a black eye.

I had arrived home after traveling in Spain for ten days, unsurprised by my mother's mind-altering moods. I had visited her the day before my departure, but dreaded—dreaded—my return, as if my absence were a sin and she was the disapproving priest doling out penance after my reappearance.

My sister Beth had been on call and it had been a common occurrence for my mother to have incidents of some greater physical impact while I was on the road. According to Beth and the caregivers, my mother had wandered down the halls with her eyes focused on her comfort shoes. My mother's depth perception was no longer what it had been when she'd caught her kids smirking, using her eyes behind her back.

Without looking up, she had bumped into another female resident who often invaded her personal space by speaking in jibber-jabber about topics my mother couldn't possibly comprehend. The two were found on the floor, my mother's short legs and arms tangled together with the other woman's long limbs. That was the story. Yet, I often overheard my mother telling various residents to shut up or stop talking. I had reason to believe she could have shoved someone aside. With brute force.

After four days, the peachy skin cuddling my mother's right eye had melted into the mix of deep greens, dusky yellows, dark purples, and blacks in an Edward Hopper painting.

She continued to yank at my slick winter coat sleeve and yell at the top of her lungs. "You stupid…." She used the same tone and insinuation she had voiced trying to keep five children in line and the threat of calling my father at the shoe store loomed large.

I jerked my arm away from her and my sleeve slipped from her grasp. "Please, Mom," I said through clenched teeth. There was a group of residents in the coffee room whose heads popped up from reading their newspapers. I had relinquished my feelings of embarrassment every time she yelled at me, but now, to protect her, I grit my teeth. "You can't keep yelling like that."

But she did.

I stared deep into her eyes. Her irises were like buoys bobbing in murky, gray water. The patch of skin over her injured eye spread out in yellow blotches. A pool of fluid floated below it.

Suddenly, I burst out laughing.

My mother's face grew red, overshadowing the yellows and blues.

"Mom, no. I wasn't laughing at you really. I wasn't." Not at her or her black eye.

"**Roooaaarrrr**," she breathed in my face.

"Ha, ha, ha, ha, ha!" I laughed back in her face as I relived a similar moment that my mother had immortalized on Polaroid paper, a snapshot taken when I was two years old after I had fallen up the steps and received a black eye. A picture for which my father would have been complicit because my mother always said, "Ette, get the camera." A photograph with the tagline of a cigarette ad written below it in my mother's handwriting. *I'd rather fight than switch.*

In 1963, the Tareyton cigarette makers had produced an ad targeted to customer loyalty. Each commercial had shown an actor doing something rebellious and rolled out its famous tagline. In one instance, an old woman was shown rocking in her chair on a porch watching over her neighborhood being razed for condos. Depicted as defiant, the old woman then uttered the slogan and turned her face, revealing a made-up black eye.

Back then, *I'd rather fight than switch* had made it as an entry into my baby photo album.

I had heard the stories from my mother about the Tareyton cigarette commercials. As a youngster, I'd never understood the tagline—or the ad. But I understood I was almost two and my mother entertained herself and the family with that photo.

I laughed harder, not at my mother's present frustration, but at her antics from long ago. In my hazy happiness, I was simply tired.

My body was limp, still living and breathing six time zones away— my spirit and stomach too. I had returned to a sick dog at home, and, after visiting some of the world's most famous museums and witnessing art come to life, the last place I wanted to be was in a memory care center where life suddenly felt like a study in my own cold, calculating patience and not warm, embracing hues.

Upon my reentry, the mother and the other residents I observed were not the mother and residents I had left behind. A half-degree had been added to the curve in my mother's stoop. I passed by rooms of residents and spotted the angel sign on a doorway. I observed a certain resident whom I often chatted with about her banker father, one of the most cogent women at the center, wilting in a wheelchair. Of course, I wondered if I was seeing things as they were, or through the lens of sadness and guilt.

The outside doors were locked due to chilly springtime temperatures. My mother pressed on the arm of the door. The alarm wailed. That didn't stop her from wanting to break out, like a jailbird in the old westerns where the key was within reach if the inmate paid attention. I circled her away from the vicinity of the back door and she hollered out a few obscenities. "Now, damn it, just leave me alone," she said to me. And I decided her black eye certainly could have come from my mother pushing someone else.

Miss Betty was penciling in answers to an acrostic puzzle. She put a pencil in her snow-white updo and shouted from her rocker, "Better watch out or she'll give you one of those too."

Didn't I know it?

Fearing another fall for my mother or that she really would take a swing at me, I kept my eyes glued on her face and one arm curved around her waist.

Twelve years ago, my parents had accompanied me to Italy. During my recent trip to Spain, I'd thought a lot about my mother and her first and only European trip. How she had bravely boarded a plane mere hours after being released from the hospital for a condition most likely anxiety-induced over an international flight. Still, she had radiated excitement.

Is that why I was pushing my mother, keeping her propped up? The memory of who she once had been in Italy? My mother and father sharing one suitcase for ten days. She, chastising him for the wine stains on his shirt. A woman huffing and puffing up the cobblestone incline, jet lag catching up to her bright eyes, toward the chapel of St. Francis of Assisi. The burnt yellow streaks of sun shining a light on her face as she had strolled through the piazzas, greeting everyone who did the same.

Spain reminded me so much of Italy. But also, not. The pastries in Spain never passed the taste test compared to my mother's cookies, cookies we no longer considered Italian because we just called them *Mom's*. The Spanish language did not come easily for me though I had been schooled in it for many years. But a quick audio course in Italian hung on in the recesses of my brain and flowed out faster than Spanish words.

Whenever I traveled to Italy without my mother, I stretched across time and centuries and terra cotta tile where our shared DNA was etched into every shape of pasta and every type of grape, and there my mother was. But I couldn't reach my mother from Spain. I couldn't feel her presence or pain.

All that came from the recollection of a photo album picture and the reflection of a yellowing bruised eye on my mother's right side and normal left eye.

My mother scrunched up her face and the diamond of skin cells thinned.

I tried to envision a youthful woman amusing herself with a picture of a two-year-old while being scorned by the older version in front of me.

Another caregiver walked past. "Jean the Bean," she called out.

My mother gazed at the young caregiver who had a fresh application of lipstick. She broke into a wide grin as she and I passed the employee and walked the same hallways we had made tracks down for years. They would have to replace the carpeting soon because of us.

My mother reached out for my hand. I was grateful to be back in the space with her and thought she was settling into her day.

"You are such a stupid, what, why, hit that over there," she said and shook my arm.

I love it when your mom is feisty, the caregivers' common response, ran through my head again.

My mother crushed my hand with more might than a Ms. World bodybuilder. If she experienced physical pain, she could rip out my hand, my arm or a leg, and keep it. If she was in emotional distress, she already possessed my heart.

I'd rather fight than switch. My mother knew who I was and who I would become when she had written the tagline across the photo. And she knew who she was, still did.

In which the chaplain sees something in my mother that I can't name.

T he center's chaplain stopped me in the Country Lane corridor of my mother's care home, where a cabinet with bunnies etched into the front caused consternation for my mother on her rounds. She had a distinct dislike for country décor.

"I've been meaning to talk to you," the chaplain said.

I flinched. Even after years of my mother living at Arden Courts with few complaints from the staff, I still wasn't sure if I should be worried when approached by someone representing authority…not to mention a higher power.

Tall with brisk blue eyes, Pastor Geoff stared intently at me. "I've noticed a change in your mom lately. Have you?"

I wondered why he was asking. What exactly had he seen? Was she more feisty or less, more loving or less?

"Yes," I finally said, leaning into the mallard duck painting hung over my shoulder. Her mind traveled further away from me to places I couldn't name, yet I felt closer to her emotionally than at any time in our relationship of fifty years. But I didn't need to share the history of my chaotic relationship with my mother to him.

He stroked his long chin, expecting me to reveal more. I could offer nothing that made sense.

"She seems more content," he said. Then he asked, "Is she on new medication?" His voice was deep with curiosity, but not concern. "Can you think of some other reason why?"

"Well, she'll soon celebrate her ninetieth birthday," I said, but that was just a date on the calendar.

I could think of only one other reason. In the midst of my mother's letting go, she was becoming something else.

Of course, my mother had always been *something else*, a phrase she'd uttered not lightly when her children talked back to her, which we did—a lot—when we were kids. She was kind enough to let us rant for brief periods of time, but if we didn't stop stretching our vocal cords, an allowance she had not been afforded growing up, she had her say with a slap or the spoon. We knew where we stood with her—and our bodies knew when we crossed a line.

As a mother, she had been a force to be reckoned with in defending her children and also offering a landing space for us when we had fallen— though only for a short time. When we grew up and overstayed our welcome, she proclaimed to anyone within shouting distance, "I love it when you kids are home, and I love it when you leave."

The week following the conversation with the chaplain, my mother attended an event where a band played more of her Italian music.

She danced and sang to "Mambo Italiano" with the proper Italian musical intonations and pretend snaps. She no longer spoke from her mind, but from a place no one could reach. She forgot how to be sad, though sometimes she became angry, scowling, throwing picture frames, kicking at medicine carts blocking her path, or when someone told her what to do. She hugged more and shrugged more.

My mother had never met a cookie she didn't devour yet she had lost some weight, as if she were shedding layers of clothes in the summer. She paced the hallways for long periods of time with a direction I didn't grasp. I, too, traveled long distances on my walks through the urban core, so I understood her need to roam, to be free of the person she didn't know she was.

But to be in my mother's presence during those times was an awe-inspiring event for me. Creases in her brow disappeared and light reflected off the smoothed-over surfaces as if she were now a tumbled, shiny agate, a word derived from the Achetes River in Italy, whose roughness had worn down. I was often brought to tears by the beauty crystallized in her face.

My mother and I existed in this state between my grief over losing her as *Mom* and her delight in finding her essential self—Vincenzella—and pulling toward a home beyond me. While I waded in sorrow, she floated atop.

My mother, known all her life as Jean, had been named *Vincenzella* after her birth father, Vincenzo Giuliani, who had lost his battle to encephalitis before he met his baby girl. Her official documents noted her birth name was *Vincenzella*, not *Vincenza* as she once had thought. That information came to light when my mother pursued a passport for our trip to Italy. She was *Vincenza* to those from "Old St. Pete's," and we called her *Vinnie* in the same way my twenty-something-year-old son called me *Netti* whenever I got a speeding ticket or dented the car. But she hadn't been *Vinnie* in years, a term mostly used by my brother. I had forgotten all about that nickname and she possibly had too.

After my father's death, I'd looked through many of my mother's personal papers, including report cards and high school reunion programs. Immediately, I'd sympathized with her. Her school and church friends, teachers and employers had rebranded my mother since birth, misspelling her first and last names, or interchanging her Italian name for her American one, a deed her own mother had welcomed.

"*Buon Compleanno*, Vincenzella," I said on the morning of my mother's birthday, greeting her with an iced snowman cookie the size of Frosty himself.

She repeated the name fluently, "Vin-chen-zella," and pronounced the *z* with a pleasing buzz. It was a song resounding through the universe. I could hear her mother's voice in hers.

While watching her consume the iced top hat and carrot nose of the snowman cookie, I revisited the conversation with the chaplain in my head. What were the reasons why my mother was changing?

My mother wasn't on any new prescription medications. Her buoyancy was a condition of where she was in her dementia, not that there were specific markers along a timeline but more like beacons in the middle of a vast ocean that might lead her to wonder, *How did I get here?* I swam to those beacons time and again, only to realize they had drifted, and so had she.

When she was stationary, I witnessed lightness emanating from her outer being. Without knowing what went on inside her mind, I suspected my mother experienced a certain clarity about her life. Shedding worldly wants and needs such as a silver watch given to her by my father or the ring that contained only January's garnet and April's diamonds—birthstones that matched her children's birthdays—she was becoming Vincenzella, a person not known to her since the day she had been named, not only a mother of five, but her essential self.

I thought back to the chaplain, someone who had witnessed more transitions than I had in my life. I wondered if he had seen what I had finally witnessed.

My mother was becoming closer to the perfect state of being.

ROCKING CHAIR REFLECTION

In which I wait for my mother to tell me what to do.

It was May. I sat in my mother's oak rocker with a green crocheted afghan cushioning my back. It was too hot, that time of year, to use the thick blanket for warmth. The warmth we both needed was outside.

Whenever the temperature rose above sixty-eight degrees, I lured my mother outside of the confines of her corridor with the promise of that first kiss of summer yet to come. I thought of the times I overworked her in physical therapy to get her moving again after a fall, so she could walk around the gardens with a slow, steady confidence and no hall monitor, once her taut legs could handle her weight and the direction of her mind. There were also times when I escorted her outside and she cussed me out.

But there was one final time when I couldn't control the outcome because I wasn't there.

My mother had been walking outside along the sidewalk and encountered another resident in her path. Or the two had been walking hand in hand or arm in arm without the other one aware. One of them pushed or pulled in the wrong direction.

Both had fallen. One landed in the mulch and was fine. My mother, unfortunately, landed on the rocks. On her hip.

The staff at my mother's had called me. The ER nurse had too. I placed a number of calls back. Contained in them were my pleas for the emergency room doctor to wait to poke and prod my mother until I could arrive at the hospital. Her health care directives stated she was not to endure excessive measures to save her life. Do Not Resuscitate. Comfort Care.

"She's a DNR/CC," I had said over and over to orderlies and receptionists on a Friday night as I scrambled through the hospital corridors.

When I'd located my mother's room, she had been resting peacefully. A short, male doctor slipped into the room. "She's a DNR/CC," I'd stated again.

He'd acknowledged that fact and went on: "We'll get her x-rays at her home. We can give her some medications for comfort before she leaves. But she doesn't seem to be in too much pain."

She had been sleeping, so it was difficult to tell.

Finally, transport had arrived and I was able to leave again and take my mother to her home, a place with people who loved her in ways I couldn't comprehend.

Now in my mother's room, her rocker was my captain's perch where I waited and rocked and imagined her rocking me in that chair. Though the stain on the chair's arms had faded from my mother's worrying palms, I didn't know for certain the age of the chair. Perhaps it had come along when my younger sisters were born. I had sold off my baby rocking chair with flattened armrests and a wide seat after Davis left for college. Sadly, it was never used for more children after my young husband was diagnosed with cancer. Had the rocker been a sleek model such as the one I sat in now, with curves in the right places for my wrists to rest, I would have kept it.

I rocked and waited. Would my mother cry out when she twisted her body? Would she wake up and smile and make my day? I collapsed into the curve of the chair, resting from the many miles my mother and I had traveled together while she lived in her care home.

I'd told my husband, "I don't want to remember Mom like this." Her body tense, possibly in a pain that she could not articulate.

But honestly, what bothered me most was that our time together in the past six years had been compressed into only moments—the good ones, the hard ones, everything in between. Those hours she and I had spent together walking through the halls and outside in the courtyard had erased the hours in my childhood when she—laughing and vibrant and young— had walked with me at a beach, the fields, our street. But I'd accepted that. What I could not accept was watching her curled up here in a bed, unable to walk, or speak, or even get mad at me.

The nurse at the care home stopped in and visited. She was new and talked about the framed photos of my mother and me that were scattered on top of cabinets and shelves like a Hollywood walk of fame. They had been taken during a Cheering for Charity event. There were frames of other residents, but there were so many of my mother because she had appeared joyful that day. In the pictures, I was smiling and full of joy too. The photographer had captured every last ounce of our togetherness.

So many important moments had transpired in my life with my mother. I recalled how she loved both my first and second husbands, my little boy, the girls now mine, our trip to Italy. But times were different, and the good moments now were extraordinary because they were simple, fleeting.

I grasped at my mother's hands. They were slender, with long nails she had once shaped and polished before her Saturday nights out with my father to Pier W for dinner, or at the Italian American Veterans Club to hang out with their Italian friends, or at the movies—her choice, never his. Her long feet and fingers were not like my stubby ones. But where once I had added up the ways in which we differed—there were so many I'd bragged about in our past—now that number diminished.

Our lives had been converging—we even shared the same cowlicks along our hairline—and I'd never noticed until now.

I spoon-fed her some pudding and imagined what I had looked like, sick in bed with measles or flu, home from school on days when she had stirred up my favorite "get better" concoction—an egg, beaten, with sugar and vanilla. *It's an old Italian thing*, she'd told me once. A while back, I had discovered a passage in a book describing a similar potion. Some days, I still made the concoction for the memory, not for an ailment or relief.

My mother didn't have a fever. There was no forehead against which to press a cold compress. I rocked and rocked and rocked. It was only eleven a.m. How would I fill my next hours when they were once filled with our walks outside? My mother looked like a deejay wearing headphones, listening to Sinatra off my iPhone. I could hear him too, and his voice was getting to me. It reminded me too much of her vitality. The lyrics about looking at the moon, not able to say goodbye, lost to the summer wind, blah, blah, blah. I abhorred him and his words at the moment. But his voice kept her calm.

Hours ago, the x-rays had been read. My mother had sustained a hip fracture. Serious enough to consider surgery—if she were someone else, younger, more spry. I was vindicated in my earlier insistence that she should be released from the hospital. But in another sense, I was condemning her.

I signed on for hospice care for her—for comfort—instead of surgery for the fractured hip. "It's not **end of life** care," I repeated guiltily to siblings and friends. There was a difference.

In all the decisions I had to make, my mother's fall had made the decision—but not the follow-through—easy for me.

Would her life be shortened now that she had fallen? Perhaps not any more than if she hadn't. Would she be comfortable in the Cadillac of wheelchairs and hospital beds? Probably so. She was already napping plenty.

Her body was worn down from being worn down. Finally, it was time for me to say **No** to more surgery or medical intervention. It was what I was best at doing.

My mother was snoring now, making sounds like the jackhammer that was used during the construction near my house. I was glad I wasn't there to hear it. The sunny weather would have brought all sorts of construction trucks to the street and the noise would have driven me insane.

My mother's room was near the television room and Dorothy's voice in *The Wizard Oz* streamed down the hallway. It was the scene where Dorothy first encountered the Wicked Witch of the West after Auntie Em's home landed on the witch's sister. *Just try to stay out of my way,* the witch said. I used to crouch behind the patchwork couch to watch the movie as a youngster, or wrap my skinny arms around my mother's belly and shut my eyes. I couldn't hide any longer. I had to face my mother and our future.

My mother lay before me, sometimes gurgling with eyes closed, sometimes staring, wide-eyed. She had not said much, but offered a few smiles and stroked my hair.

"I'm here," I reminded her out loud and plastered my arms to her torso, unwilling to let go. "We'll get through this together."

Someone turned up the volume on the television. The theme song from *The Wizard of Oz* drifted in from the other room.

We had been on a yellow brick road to see the Wizard, my mother and I. At times we were each other's Dorothy, or the Good Witch and Bad Witch. We were the Cowardly Lion filled with fear, the scatterbrained Scarecrow and the Tin Man looking for love. And the Lollipop Kids—two short girls, singing side by side. Who didn't want to be them?

And now we had arrived at a point in our journey where Toto tugged back the green curtain.

Like Dorothy, my mother never needed the Wizard to pull the levers nor Glinda, the Good Witch, to transfer the ruby slippers to her feet. She knew the way. Her feet still knew the way even if she no longer could walk.

For once in my life, I had to listen to her, and let her make her way home.

I would be in the rocker, waiting.

In which I learn the meaning of **meaning**.

"You gotta have heart to do this job," Sieta said. Sieta was one of my mother's caregivers and her long braids, wound like those of an African queen, and topped off by a bun at the crown, swung in the air as she turned away to pour my mother a glass of juice.

I tried to spoon lumpy cream of wheat through my mother's pursed lips and wondered whether my mother's current life had meaning. How would I define **meaning**? How would she? Would she feel there was meaning after being confined, imprisoned by dementia and a useless hip that would sway to Sinatra no more? And how would the assembly of caregivers, those who surrounded her and fussed over her every need, feel? Any different from me?

My mother was dressed in baggy pajamas instead of her usual street clothes. She was on a low dose of pain medication, but while she could chew and swallow, she seemed to be in a fog from the narcotics. At the intersection of pain medication for comfort after her hip fracture versus a state of constant wakefulness and distress, I had turned to drugs for my mother.

My mother finished her breakfast. As she nodded off, I wheeled her into the courtyard. The day was warm with rain just spittin'. Before the broken hip, she would have screamed at me for getting her wet. But now, she didn't. I chuckled a bit, getting away with something.

Having obtained my driver's permit for her unwieldy wheelchair, I now steered her outside at all hours. I was more determined than ever to make her days refreshing ones. I fed her breakfast al fresco and we picnic-lunched with nippy ants.

Wherever she was in her disease, I wanted her to have the prickle of sunshine on her arms and a whoosh of fresh air in her face. Wherever she was going, I wanted her to have some sense of the world until the end.

Did that give meaning to her life?

I returned to the theories my husband and I had batted about all week following the fracturing of her hip. Was she leading a meaningful life?

Was the honest answer, *No, she is not?*

Sieta's words about *heart* floated back into my head.

In the days after my mother's accident and subsequent confinement to a wheelchair, I sobbed and embraced the caregivers every time I scurried in and out of her room, the kitchen and the outdoors. I thanked each woman—and they were ninety-nine percent women—for whatever they had done, for whatever they were about to do, especially as it related to my mother's bathing and cleansing. Self-care had been utmost to her, and therefore important to me.

I had always shied away from talking about my mother's incontinence out of respect for her. Over the years, she had undergone several surgeries and possessed a digestive tract that never cooperated with what she wanted to eat. And she always wanted to eat, except when she had been younger and gone on a grapefruit diet.

Her early years with dementia were spent in shame after losing control of her bowels and soiling her clothing in public, or worse, church. Her condition had been the cause of much hardship for my mother and anyone who cared for her. She and I had often found ourselves twisted and tangled in a cramped bathroom stall at a Bob Evans, a city park or even in my own home, changing out her pants or socks into an article of clothing that belonged to my husband or son, eventually transitioning to Depend underwear.

As my mother's dementia had worsened, her brain lost all bladder and bowel control. If I could have taken one condition away in all this, it would have been that embarrassment. I would have chosen for her to keep her dignity.

Yet, never once did any caregiver of my mother's complain. They jumped or rushed to change her clothes to keep her comfortable. Not doing so would lead to a bladder infection that led to seizures that led to…that led to.

Back in bed, my mother lay with her legs curled into herself, a flower pulling her petals inward, unwilling to extend them for fear of hip pain. Two of my mother's regular caregivers, Janice and Angel, bathed her ninety-year-old body. Her shower would come tomorrow with hospice help. For now, warm, worn washcloths tickled her tummy and the short arms and the legs she kept pulled in to her core. It was most sacred what I witnessed as Janice tenderly ran the cloth along my mother's legs, under her arms and beneath her single breast.

I melted to see my mother so vulnerable, and was humbled by a level of devotion that I had not accomplished. Surely these women were angels.

A former boss of mine once said, "Never ask anyone to do a job you wouldn't do yourself." That was my mantra for my mother's care. I did things when I had to, but also had the support of the caregivers who performed a job few would have the courage to do.

Janice, her smooth face crinkled with worry, told me to text her while she was on vacation if my mother's condition changed or worsened.

Kre, who grinned, her white teeth gleaming, leaned in and said, "Hello Mamma." My mother beamed back.

Lakeisha, once employed on staff, now visited my mother as a hospice caregiver and my mother's face lit up in Lakeisha's presence. My mother loved her sassy attitude.

Jayna stressed out if she couldn't change the residents immediately, yet in other external settings, there were residents who lay about all day in sopping sheets and undershirts.

My mother was best at mothering and the women at Arden Courts— Jayna, Kre, Lakeisha, Janice, Becky, Cleo, Valerie, Suzy, Sieta, Angel, Tiffany, Angela, Bobbi, (and so many other givers of care for one woman's body and mind)—were like daughters to her. I so desperately wanted them to know my mother as the woman she had once been, the one I was still pining for.

Yet they were content to love and care for the woman in front of them. While I, as family, often saw her as diminished, her caregivers saw her as someone growing into who she was.

Janice plated the meals for lunch, ladled gravy over the potatoes, knew who wanted cereal for lunch instead of chicken, who needed ketchup or Diet Coke, who still required a nap and who just needed to see her serene countenance.

Her face fresh with light, Janice found my mother and me outside. With somewhat of a southern accent, she said, "Here you are my friend," and set the plastic plate on the table.

My mother gazed up at her with the adoration of a second-grader taking communion. She used to echo *friend* back. Now, she was silent.

I jumped in, and said, "Friend," instead.

Janice's actions acutely demonstrated a deep devotion. And while I bragged my mother was one of her favorites, Janice lavished on all residents the same love and attention anyone would wish for when turning eighty-four, ninety or one-hundred-and-three. The staff breathed a culture that adhered to this notion.

On Mother's Day, a week after my mother's fall, I had woken to a touching email from Becky, the activities director. Over our chats, Becky and I determined she had started work at the care home two months after my mother had arrived. She had observed my recent struggles to cope with my mother:

> *Happy Mother's Day. I am thinking of you today and standing with you in spirit. I read your blog today. I don't know what your particular spiritual beliefs are, but my experience as a witness to many last years of living is that, far beyond the time people are able to communicate, they are able to love and accept love. Your mother has been absolutely blessed by the fierce, unwavering, unconditional love you have given her in the time I have known you both. Please know you are not alone. Lean on those people you trust. Take care of yourself. I'll be there—and Janice will be there—for your mom through the end.*

The email was proof of the commitment of the women at a place I generally referred to as *Mom's*. Proof that we were all capable of loving with no genetic strings attached.

What was the definition of **meaning**? Something intangible that knew no bounds?

With the tip of her tongue, my mother pushed at a spoonful of brown potatoes and gravy and clamped her lips tight. Lunch was over. I handed in her plate like a kid in a junior high cafeteria.

Was my mother leading a life with meaning?

Thirteen years earlier, my mother had undergone hip replacement surgery. She had prepped and cooked her meals and frozen them before her operation. Now, in her weakened state, she required more care than ever before.

I choked up thinking of all that had happened. Yet I knew my mother wouldn't want to remember me weeping as I stood over her, tears streaming down my face—*Oh, 'Net, you take things too hard*—so instead I blinked my eyes and imagined her dancing the tarantella and singing "C'e La Luna Mezz'o Mare" so many years back in my godmother Sarah's kitchen. I began to smile as my mother opened her eyes and whispered, "Hey you," then went back to sleep. This was all I needed – to feel seen and loved by her for a moment. Was it enough for a mother to know she had given her own daughter's life meaning?

If this end was not what I wanted for my mother, the best I could hope for was she had been welcomed, raised, and loved by the women (and occasional men) who had surrounded her. Her life gave others work filled with meaning, and hearts filled with love.

MY MOTHER'S LISTS

In which my mother's lives begin to add up.

M y mother was a famed listmaker. *Groceries for Thanksgiving. What to Pack for Italy. Dinner for New Year's Day. Church Cleaning Chores. Four Weeks before Easter. Easter Menu.* Her work in the kitchen was unparalleled because of her endless lists.

Now, I was driving a wheelchair in which my mother would be confined for the rest of her life. I pushed at it from behind into the great outdoors and rampant humidity while in my head, I ran down a list of my own—the physical obstacles my mother had overcome in her ninety years of being:

1. *Hip replacement.*
2. *Thyroid malfunctioning when her incompetent doctor suggested calling hospice.*
3. *Removal of her appendix and some other little thing the doctor said was blocked and caused her stomach to blow up the size of a basketball.*
4. *Three seizures.*
5. *Shingles.*
6. *A fall ending with a black eye.*
7. *Eating flowers and leaves, the real ones and fake ones.*
8. *Swallowing soap and nearly needing a tracheotomy.*

Her record of medical speed bumps encountered in her long life, excluding the overarching dementia, read like a multiple-choice answer on an MCAT exam.

The house doctor always sought me out after examining her, following any one of those medical hiccups.

He clicked his pen and said, "Your mother definitely has nine lives." I never doubted that, as it was true of so many individuals with dementia.

"The hospice chaplain said she might have thirteen," I said.

"And she just goes on smiling at me today."

He was young, handsome, of Indian descent. Yes, my mother would smile at him.

As I circled around the courtyard, I added up more of her challenges. Anything that kept my mind off the fact she was now confined to bed or a wheelchair and losing the last of whatever number life she was on. She slept through lunch. And she was losing weight, but not enough to be too alarmed, only enough to take notice.

Now there was an obvious item to add to the list. After my mother had fallen, the nurse had said to me, "She was outside, just lying there, smiling, on the rocks," and the Neil Diamond song "Love on the Rocks" played in my head each time I thought about her accident that resulted in a fractured hip.

One incident I'd missed on my mental list. My mother's breast cancer. She and my father had informed my husband about her diagnosis but hid it from me when I had been living in Oregon and had given birth to Davis four weeks premature.

And that morning, I had been told about my mother's most recent challenge. Deep blood clots had formed in her leg from not moving her body. She had now crossed the threshold of Ironwoman designation.

The sun beat down on the concrete. A *whoosh* of heat curled up from the sidewalk and seared my exposed toes. If I could feel it, so could my mother.

I parked the wheelchair beneath the shade of an umbrella and retrieved headphones from my purse. While my mother was sleeping on the outside, on the inside her ears might still be wide-awake. I placed the headphones over her ears' long lobes. That day, I picked out Italian mandolin music. If there was a heaven, there would be many mandolins, a true Italian instrument, playing to her satisfaction.

My focus was drawn to a raised flower box as a few musical notes slipped out of my mother's ear buds. I leaned back and my eyelids closed by themselves, batting away tears.

How hard had I worked at keeping my mother safe, healthy? I'd tried to steer her away from chomping on the plastic or real flowers or plants that dotted the winding paths of the courtyard or interior landscape of her care home. Except I had let her eat the tiny tomatoes which would flourish sooner rather than later this summer. We'd always picked one or two, so she could taste of her ancestry. Away from any pain or hurt.

I thought of my siblings, of being a child of Jean's. Delving into the list of emotional or psychological aches of hers was like devouring a year's worth of Lifetime movies, with so many obstacles to overcome:

1. *Her birth father dying before she knew him.*
2. *Her first-born son dying two days after birth.*
3. *Her mother dying while my mother was in her thirties.*
4. *The breakup of the family shoe store business
   and my father's loss of a livelihood.*
5. *A son-in-law succumbing to cancer.*
6. *A daughter surviving cancer.*
7. *A second daughter surviving cancer.*
8. *My father's death.*
9. *A third daughter battling alcoholism…We always kept our
   secrets from her five years out.*

The mandolins didn't calm me, only her. I bounced my knees and wanted to move again. My arm muscles twitched as I gripped on the wheelchair handles, located at too high a height for me. Who needed a workout when I could push her and this unwieldy chair? What I needed were distractions.

I propelled her forward in the wheeled contraption over every crack known to me in those sidewalks, over all the gradual inclines and bumps and declines, into a murky future.

Squirrels escaped through a few slivers in the base of the whitewashed fence. I looked up and around at a neighbor's house over the fence. What was the neighbor thinking? Was the neighbor making his own list of residents he had come to know—and miss?

I was tired of exploring all the square inches that made up the space around the courtyard, and returned to study the flowers in their beds and pots. I'd always looked forward to the flowers that bloomed each spring and summer. What would grow there once my mother was gone? What would die? It was a meditation on the residents themselves—and on my mother. Who would blossom again in the spring? Who would fail to thrive?

The Irish poet, Michael Longley, wrote a poem, "The Ice Cream Man," for the owner of an ice cream parlor who had been murdered. In the verses, the poet drew parallels between the ice cream flavors in the shop and that of wildflowers in the Burren where he had been cataloging them. I no longer carried in live flowers to my mother because of her tendency to eat them. We wheeled and wheeled in an endless circle of life and death and remembering and not. Like the poet naming ice cream flavors, I named for my mother the flowering plants in the landscape beds: *Verbena, astilbe, hydrangea, hosta, salvia, Russian sage, the tiny yellow stars on the tomato plant, sweet potato vine, mint, pansy, sweet Melissa, lavender, rosemary, black-eyed Susan, Asiatic lily.*

There was no response from her.

I needed rest. My mind needed a rest. I stopped circling beneath the canopy of a birch tree. Janice carried out our lunch plates.

My mother opened her eyes. She stared into a faraway horizon. I tried spooning a few bites of mashed chicken into her mouth but she hacked on the lumps. I handed her a cup filled with a blue sports drink. While she drank, I looked up into the cloudless sky.

Only for a second.

"Eeeck!"

She was wide-eyed now as the drink dribbled down her chin and flowed across her Jolly Rancher blue-raspberry-colored top, one that matched the hue of the sports drink.

I grabbed the napkin. "Mom, I'm so sorry. Let's try that again." It was a maxim we shared, one that captured our relationship succinctly when I was younger and now. I sopped up the droplets and swept the cornbread crumbs off her pant legs. Laughing through tears, I felt grateful we were still prone to our comedic routines. Or at least I was.

From my mother's right side—her good side for her hair part and hearing and eyesight—I said, "I don't know what the future holds for you, Mom." The tip of my nose touched hers.

Softly, she said, "I don't either."

I curled a short lock of hair around her ear, trying to imagine what my mother's last wish for her life on this earth might be. Reading one final book or a column of Erma Bombeck's, or watching *Cat on a Hot Tin Roof* with Paul Newman one more time? Eating dinner with the whole family back at our house in Amherst?

But last wishes were always tinged with regrets and my mother was not a regretful person.

Our eyes were wide now, both sets dripping wet. Were hers wet from allergies? Mine were wet from grief. Her eye color, which oddly matched her bluish top, had been shifting in tint and depth. *When we die, do we finally get the color of eyes we always coveted? And the clarity too?*

I brushed at wisps of her gray and white strands sparkling in the sun and fluttering like butterflies in the breeze. I cupped her scalp, still clinging to its thinning hair, in the palm of my hand.

"Don't you dare!" She swatted my hand away.

There she was, her face scrunched up again. My feisty mother.

She would finish her own list.

WHAT TO WEAR

In which
I give my mother
permission to leave.

I didn't know what to wear the day I thought my mother would die. Summer had kicked in. The rains dropped in and out of the clouds, as if from a dripping showerhead. I first slipped into a flimsy Target skirt made from t-shirt material I might roll up and toss in a suitcase and somehow unroll it wrinkle-free on the other side of the TSA line. Respectability, at least the appearance of it, had been important to my mother.

If she were dying, maybe I should wear a skirt.

The day before, I had sat for hours at my mother's bedside after noting many changes. She had tugged at her reddening ear lobes in a Carol Burnett sort of way. With her tongue, she'd pushed out food I fed her. No to banana pudding? No to Busken cookies? Swallowing became a chore for which there was no reward. Her agitation, with eyes mostly clamped shut, moved to a new level. And when I left her side for an appointment with my hairstylist—she would have approved—and returned, her agitation had scaled another story or two. Animal noises of agony came out of her lips. We thought we were managing the pain from her fractured hip, but perhaps not.

Janice had transferred my mother from the wheelchair to bed after lunch to see if the change might offer her relief. After several more hours and a few consultations with me, the caregivers called the hospice nurse instead. I couldn't bear the agony of her pain. I had a sworn-duty to protect her from that.

As she had squirmed around in bed, something notable had been happening. There was a process that occurred when the heart no longer pumped blood effectively to the extremities, in particular the feet and hands, and the skin became discolored. It was called by another name, but I called it *dappling*. Dappling sounded more heavenly, less medical and cold.

The nurse had suggested I call my siblings. It was finally time.

But it wasn't.

Then came the next day. Fully-dressed, my skirt flew up behind me as I shuttled between my office and bedroom, which were both on the second floor of our Italianate-style town home, dashing off emails and writing notes in between blow-drying my hair. I feared letting go of my own life while acknowledging that soon I would have to let go of my mother's.

As I stepped on the porch to water my plants, a shot of rain came down and soaked the petunias and coleus and other miscellaneous flora barely surviving my inattention. I stopped long enough to thank my father, the gardener, who seemed to be saying to me, "Be with Mom. I'll take care of the plants."

Inside, I scrambled back and forth in the hallways to locate chargers and plugs for all my electronic devices. Cords dangled from my arms as if I were an octopus trying to carry everything I might need.

Hurrying back to my closet, I spotted a pair of folded jeans atop a laundry basket full of clean clothes. When had I even done the laundry? Or had Mark? To save myself the task of hanging the jeans, I snatched them up. I yanked off my skirt and wriggled my way into comfort. I needed a different approach. If my mother was dying, I needed my work jeans. They made me feel confident and were time-tested, like the relationship with my mother. The skirt lay crumpled on the ground.

Soon I was in my mother's room, where I sat for another round of fourteen hours in a setting where her life had been downsized, one containing all the belongings she needed within a tiny space, with a half bath to boot. She had traveled a long way from her home on Lincoln Street down the interstate only to land here.

For a while, a rosy blush covered her face, a result of the medications. Lakeisha, her hospice nurse, gave her a sponge bath and rubbed a lavender-scented lotion into her skin. "Oh, don't Jean the Bean smell good."

"Lakeisha, so good to see you." I loved that woman, any woman who came into my sight that day.

"Thanks, Miss Annette. I'm glad to be here." And I knew she really was. She turned away from me and asked of my mother, "Now what should we wear?"

My mother's classic outfit of a cream blouse, black skirt or pants hadn't been part of her wardrobe in so long, though she probably would have wanted to wear something more proper than what I suggested. "How 'bout that salmon-colored, flowered, sequined one? It's her favorite," I said, wanting my mother at least to wear a complementary color palette for what lay ahead.

I went to the closet. "The shirt isn't in here."

I couldn't believe it. That missing shirt represented everything I did for my mother: sweater shopping, fingernail clipping, disposable underwear buying, everything the caregivers did too, yet we couldn't find it anywhere. She was getting cold. Not even Janice could find the shirt. We all gave up.

"That pink one will have to do," I said. Plus the pink shirt had a sheath of lace that resembled Italian tatting and I found it strangely fitting.

At the end of the evening, after the dinner hour, my mother's agitation increased again. She breathed in moans and groans. Her chest rose and stopped. Fell and stopped. The breathing pattern, too, had a name. *Cheyne-Stokes* breathing. Everything about her dying now had a name.

"Is this it?" I asked Stephanie, the young, night hospice aide. "Should I call my sister Beth?" Where was she? What time did she say she was coming back? I couldn't remember anything except what was in front of me, and even that I was struggling to remember. I tried to think of something deep and essential to say to my mother, but I was speechless in that moment.

Counting, I kept track of my mother's breaths and the time of her last medicine administration.

"She needs more, more of something," I said quietly.

Stephanie agreed, her short bangs waving as she nodded. She tracked down the nurse supervisor who called the doctor for a new set of orders.

Stephanie was a little young for what had been my experience with hospice aides. "How is it that you came to work for hospice?" I asked while we waited.

"I was a really young mom, went back to school with two little kids at home."

Her compassion stemmed not from age, but perhaps from necessity, like mine had.

We continued to talk more about the direction of her career and in the back of my mind, I thought of how life carries on. Stephanie would leave that night and tuck her little children in bed. I would leave later too. I would start my car and drive to my home in the city and kiss my husband goodnight. My life would go on.

An hour later my mother was repositioned. She rested, surrounded by pillows on top of a marshmallow bed.

I relaxed, but not all the way, wondering if I had held on too tight for too long with too much of my own strength, crushing my mother's. What if it had been not my strength, but my regrets instead? What if I said goodbye without all the fussing and kissing and locking my arms around her? Could I let her go?

My sister Beth arrived and stayed for the hour. She was reluctant to leave. I was too, until Stephanie wisely said, "If you're meant to be here when your mother dies, then you'll be here. If you're not, it's not meant to be."

No one had ever counseled me on *how to leave* throughout the other deaths I'd encountered. But it was true. If my mother needed permission from the living to leave, so too did the living need permission to go.

After Beth left, it came my turn to say goodnight or whatever I intended to say.

The problem was, I had already said all I knew to say the night before. I'd spoken to my mother about reuniting with her baby son, the one she had only held for two days. I'd talked to her about her mother, her birth father, my father, Devin, and everyone else whose life had meaning to her, but was now dead. I wasn't sure if that comforted her or not, but she was the one who toted us to the cemetery every Sunday when we were kids, so I had that evidence as backup.

That night, I switched my goodbye theme from death to life, from the others to her and me. It was the only topic on which I was an expert.

In my mother's more cognitive state, she had occasionally uttered phrases to me: *Hey, that's funny…Hey, I like you…Hey, I don't like you.* But my favorite, the one that played in my ear, was *Hey, we're a pretty good team.* In her melodic voice, she would hit a pitch like Laura Petrie in *The Dick Van Dyke Show* and laugh long at her perceived joke.

I was seated on my mother's right side in her rocker, which had been wedged between her bed and the wall. Sinatra hadn't sung all day, a welcome relief for me. Instead, I played Women in Jazz, The Boswell Sisters, Ella Fitzgerald, and some old Nancy Wilson. But I queued up Frankie once more.

A few lines seemed to be disappearing on her face as if she were more relaxed.

Through incessant tears, I said, "Mom, we've made a good team. Of course, nothing like you and Dad, but still, we did all right." I rubbed her now bony hands, looking at the brown spots which I used to joke were her ink spots, and placed one of her mottled hands over a tanned one of mine, waiting earnestly for her powerful grip where she might mash my fingers between hers and my wedding band. Her hand remained limp.

I rubbed my hands along her cheeks, those too slowly vanishing. "Mom, if you're really listening, and I believe you are, because I'm speaking into your good ear, know this."

I paused, struggling to say the right words—the right, final ones.

"We've been on this path for a long time, and it's been filled with so many joyful moments and amazing views. We've walked the Oregon Coast together, we've walked Italy, Seattle, vineyards, Cincinnati, Amherst, lakes, oceans, rivers." The list was endless. "And of course, here. All the miles we've walked." I imagined we had covered several hundred miles at her care home, not easy to accomplish on those three acres of quiet set back from a bustling four-lane road.

She sipped in several breaths, her cheeks hollowing out more, and held another few. The blanket rippled as she breathed.

"This path separates. You can see it up ahead." I could hardly utter the lines that came next about me and this woman I had grown to love fiercely. "You and I, we have to separate."

I sat beside her, weeping. That would be her final image of me, one with hair strands plastered to my temples while the rest of my locks were clipped at the nape of my neck.

"But nothing, nothing will be more perfect than where you will be walking," I said. I wanted to give her a description of a Thomas Kinkade painting, the golden glow casting light on the pastel colored woods or of a da Vinci painting of the Virgin of the Rocks. But the only image that came to mind was the one solidified on the sidewalks of her care home as we strolled through gardens of sunflowers and magnolia trees.

I was leaving in two days for my son's college graduation and the Oregon Coast. All week, I had said to Mark, "If Mom dies while I'm gone, I'll kill her." I never said it to her. But we had journeyed to that far edge together and damn, I wanted to be with her when she made the leap.

"And my path? I'm going to Oregon. Again. You know, I was always leaving you for Oregon."

I lay my head next to my mother's in some twisted yoga pose. The flattened top of her head fit squarely into the right corner made by the crook in my neck. The scent of lavender mingling with life tickled my nose. I gazed up at the darkened ceiling and fell into her body's warmth. That same warmth I wanted her to feel. "On your path, Mom, I see the rays cutting through the trees. It's your sunshine. And you can go, Mom. You can go find the sun."

I released her body from my own death grip, and patted her chest, near her heart. I kept my hand there, tapping on a familiar bump along the top of her breastbone called the manubrium. I had the same bump. I would always know where to find her.

That night, I left with a lightness in my heart. I had offered a way forward for both of us, a key to unlock the gates of whatever coveted land lay ahead.

At home, I dropped my jeans on the floor next to the skirt. I would wear the skirt the next day, I promised myself, too tired to pick up anything but my feet and hoist them into bed.

"MOM IS OUTSIDE"

In which
I get what I want
for my mother.

E arly morning. I stumbled through the unlit bathroom. The skirt not worn the day before lay mangled beneath the night's ripped jeans.

When I was a kid, I'd hated wearing skirts and dresses. I was a tomboy and my legs always looked like tree trunks beneath the canopy of a skirt hem, legs like those of my mother's mother. I chose to wear pants. Still did. When reaching for comfort, I aimed for the hangers with pants. In the writing world, those who plotted out their story were called *plotters*, and those who operated by instinct were called *pantsers*. I was the latter in writing and in life.

I wiggled into running gear, poured my coffee with eyes partially closed and slurped it down. My legs felt heavy as an elephant's as I left the house for a quick morning walk around and around Washington Park. I stayed in close proximity to my street. I thought the fear of separation from my mother had dissipated, thanks to the hospice worker's wisdom—whether I was meant to be with my mother or not—but it hadn't.

Once back home, I took a quick shower. Everything was quick that morning, including the decision to seize the skirt and writhe my way into it.

I lugged all my bags, one filled with headphones, nail clippers, nail polish, things I had always carried to my mother for our "spa" days, along with my bag of electronics.

At the care home, Janice was running a warm cloth over my mother's forehead and bathing her with a soap that evoked the lilac bushes of my childhood home. We didn't exchange words, only looks. What was a good look or a sad one? We both wanted the same thing.

I went off to the bathroom then wandered outside. I needed energy. My mother and I used to take in early summer mornings, walking outside without purpose. We had always shared the same sidewalk, as she clutched my arm for dear life and I grimaced, holding her dear life in return. But now I was alone.

The sky revealed a blue boldness. "Not a cloud anywhere," I said to myself as if my mother were at my side. I walked back toward the courtyard near my mother's room and caught a glimpse of what had always caught her eye—the shiny tin roof vent.

I headed to the nearby bench, our morning bench where we had sat in the summer sun beneath the eaves, catching sunlight only on our legs. Metal chimes rang as the breezes picked up. I sat and listened for a while, listening to my mother's voice in my head.

When I entered my mother's room again, she appeared cozy and restful, this time wearing her favorite shirt. The shirt was the color of sunset, a dreamy blend of oranges and pinks and a few sequins added for glimmer. "You found it?" I squealed, excited to find something to celebrate.

Janice beamed. "I tracked it down this morning."

I lifted up the sheet to observe my mother's feet. They were no longer dappled with purple. Instead, they were purple all over. Her blood was leaving her and she was leaving me.

Deb, a jovial hospice nurse, arrived shortly after. In between chatting about her chickens, she fussed with taking my mother's vitals, and charted her findings silently.

She rolled the blood pressure cuff up and I knew before she even looked at me.

"I asked the nurse to change her meds to every hour," she said.

"Okay," I nodded in agreement—and understanding.

A current of cool air, sneaking in from the window Janice had opened, circled the room, sending a wave of goose bumps along my bare legs.

Soon, Becky joined. "That fresh air sure feels good."

"These places should install garage doors in residents' rooms, like the doors they have in breweries nowadays," I said. "Then anyone could easily gain access to the outside." We all laughed, but saying that gave me an idea.

Seated in the rocker, I twisted toward the sunny window where the blue skies teased me, then directed my gaze back to my mother's doorway, like a carpenter evaluating its width.

"Wouldn't it be great if we could roll that hospital bed right through the door for Mom to get outside?"

There was an awkward moment of silence until Deb said, "We can do that. If that's what the family wants."

I was family. It's what I wanted. It was what I had always wanted. To be outside in the sun with my mother.

No other options had to be considered. No physical malady forced my hand. It was the easiest decision I had made in the years of overseeing my mother's care.

In a matter of minutes, five staff members, including Janice, swarmed in. They wrapped my mother in her sheets as if she were a *bambina*, and cradled her in their arms as they slid her across the bed and into a reclining wheelchair, while I handed off pillows for the various gaps between her and the chair.

Like the ground crew of an airplane, we moved my mother to the exact spot where the sunlight breached the magnolias and the birch trees, where flickers of sun swept the sidewalk. The path split into a "Y" and, every time we had walked there, my mother had tugged one way and I had tugged the other, because my way was the long way and her way led to the dead end.

In her makeshift carriage, my mother was outside. Deb and I settled in chairs between patches of light and shade, with my mother's face visible to the sun. I texted my siblings and my husband. *Mom is outside.*

I was elated.

Could she feel it? Did she know it?

Mom is outside, I chanted to myself in my head as I selected my Sinatra playlist to shuffle on my iPhone.

The sun that day was tinged with enough heat to make me believe I could live outside forever. My mother, too. But soon, the sun's intense beams hit on my face and seared through to my insides. "She's probably not comfortable," I said and Deb nodded. We maneuvered her chair back into the flecks of light through the trees.

A nurse came by to administer my mother's medication at ten a.m.

"Yes. More," I said in a low voice. It would be soon.

My sister Beth arrived, as if on cue.

In the space between idle chitchat and the quiet buzzing of bugs, and Sinatra singing "Blue Skies," Deb said under her breath, "Annette and Beth. Hold your Mom's hand."

My mother's breathing had been labored and slowed. And now halted.

Beth and I gazed at each other sadly then resolutely grasped our mother's hands in ours. We waited. And waited. And waited.

My heart pounded. My mother's belly, the one that filled with *her music* and Italian cookies over the years, didn't rise. Her chest didn't fall.

Did she? Had she?

"10:33 a.m.," Deb called out, as Sinatra's words to "We Just Couldn't Say Goodbye" wove their way into the moment.

There beneath the quiet skies of a summer day, my mother became a songbird set free.

Vincenzella Jean Giulani Januzzi was no longer bound by the confines of the wheelchair, the dark recesses where her mind might have wandered lost, released from what society might see—an aging woman with dementia— and certainly liberated from my need to push her to be all that she could be in her disease.

After my mother's last moment savoring the Earth's sun, my sister and I gathered in the courtyard with the chaplain and our husbands, who had been on hold waiting to be called, to lift our mother up in prayer. We said the *Our Father* and the *Hail Mary* and I shared a story about the first prayer I learned from her, a prayer for my dead brother:

"Her firstborn, David, died two days after his birth. So when we knelt as a family to say prayers before the sewing machine turned altar, we said the *Our Father*, the *Hail Mary* and a little prayer Mom had written. So, I'll just say it now."

I took a moment to catch my breath, then continued.

"Please, Baby David, watch over us and help us to be a good, kind and loving family."

Pastor Geoff looked up toward the sky and said in a miraculous tone, "She's completed her final act of mothering."

Before the staff carried the body away, I inhaled the fragrant smell of lilacs from lotion applied to her neck only an hour earlier. But my mother also smelled of longing. I patted her soft, drawn-in cheeks, ones I would never stroke again, cheeks I had nuzzled up to time and again whenever I had greeted or left her. Nuzzling was how we stayed connected, how we knew one another, through our touch and scents.

Tears in my eyes, I looked at my skirt and noticed the goose bumps running up and down my legs.

Yes. We had made a pretty good team. She had completed her last act as my mother. And I had completed my last act as her daughter.

Epilogue

In which I discover what is left behind in my mother's room.

"Nun-uh," Janice said, shaking her head with a sad smile, her hair extensions shaking too. She was seated at the front desk, giving the receptionist a lunch break. "I still won't let Derek put anyone in that room."

The room she referred to was beyond the second secure door. It was the room closest to the caregiver station down the corridor known as Country Lane.

It was the room that had belonged to my mother.

My mother had died five months earlier, and with the daylight waning in November, her spirit still cast a long shadow over the caregivers and courtyards that had bolstered her life for so many years.

And a long shadow over me.

I stopped in that day to assuage my guilt. I had committed to visiting. I would come back, I'd promised. I needed to know if the little woman with a superhero grip who had beckoned me in all those years would do so once more.

"Every time the number comes up," Derek said as he walked out from behind a desk, "I just pass it up." Derek, a member of the marketing staff, was tall with dark hairs grazing across his chin and upper lip. He snapped his long fingers and smiled at Janice and me.

He was referring to room number 13. In a life where my mother won only the booby prize in pinochle and we joked about the long-standing era of our family's Januzzi jinx after a cook at a Denny's restaurant quit his job and walked out of the restaurant right after our family had ordered, she was given the extraordinary luck of finding loving caregivers in a room with an unlucky number.

They didn't mean it about the unassigned room and were just trying to be nice, I thought, staring in Janice's eyes shielded by long lashes, her round face framed by a hairstyle that changed on a daily basis. But her smile had stayed true to its width and her white teeth shone through as a testimony to her mixture of sadness and sweetness that crossed her mind when thinking of my mother. She of all the caregivers was most unable to put into words her unexpected love for a woman she had only expected to be her duty.

Talking to Janice and Derek, I leaned over the desk, my feet aching from the black patent heels on my feet. I was better dressed than I would have typically been when visiting with my mother. I used to wear jeans and a sweatshirt, which often led my mother to tease me. Or she would eye my black sweater from Target with fake gemstones along the collar, and say, "Oh, so high class."

I had felt my mother's presence as I'd entered into the warmth of her former home. The waves of laughter and sadness taken in over the years rippled through me. My mother's voice rang along the hallways that lay behind the secure door and thrummed in my ears. I so wanted her back roaming those same hallways, moving furniture, making nice or mean with the people she passed.

I had visited three times since her death, each with a few more weeks passing between visits, separating me further from my mother and our past. When I drove up the long driveway and veered left or right, I looked for familiar cars and was met with the sight of Janice's navy blue sedan. It was the sign I had once always looked for—then I'd known my mother was happy.

Standing in the foyer, I saw the flickering ghosts of caregivers, staff, my sister and me, all following my mother on a gurney in the tradition of Arden Courts to accompany the body as it left the premises for the final time. I was yanked back to that day she died.

My mother had stopped breathing around ten-thirty a.m. and by noon, as we all had stood in the parking lot around the hearse, the scene took on a golden Hollywood shimmer. We shielded our eyes, eyes blurred by salt and memory, eyes adjusting from the darkened hallways we had occupied only minutes before as the funeral home escort prepared for my mother's leaving.

Outside with my mother placed in the hearse, we had listened to Jana, the director, speak about Jean the Bean. Suzanne, the cheery receptionist, shared how my mother "really gave it to the Elvis impersonator" and that memory had rocketed my mother to the top of her list of favorite residents. As part of the staff's goodbye, Suzanne stepped up to read a passage from Khalil Gibran. *For what is it to die, but to stand naked in the wind and to melt into the sun?*

I recalled how beneath the sheets falling into my mother's suddenly hollowed cheeks, her tiny, cold body, still holding on to her pixie-cut hairs, was melting into the sun. I imagined her melting away from me like clarified butter, turning into or toward more perfect matter. She no longer was mother, wife or resident with dementia. She was her self.

I, too, would have melted at that prospect.

On the day of my mother's death, the director had asked the group of caregivers if they had anything more to share. Felicia, a large-boned woman, slowly moved away from the crowd of caregivers standing under the eaves. "I just remember Jean and I used to sing *Unforgettable* and she would finish singing..."

Before Felicia could say more, the skinny hearse driver—who could have passed for a Harlem Globetrotter—inched away from his post at the back of the car. Our focus was on him as he had started the engine. A loud crackling came from the car stereo and through it, notes of Nat King Cole soon drifted, singing "Unforgettable."

I had waved my arms to rally the caregivers. We'd circled together and stood shoulder-to-shoulder, where the burden of my mother's care had been evenly spread, staff to daughter to caregiver, arms around each other.

For the final time, we lifted my mother in song.

Later after the hearse drove away, I had walked back inside with my sister Beth. My feet in flip-flops felt heavy. My cell phone rang and rang. There was much work ahead of me before I could mourn my mother: A son's college graduation that weekend, flying out of town the next morning, a funeral to plan, financial accounts to rectify and the duty in front of me—cleaning out her room.

"Do it now because you won't be able to come back for a while," Jana had said earlier, patting my back in a maternal fashion though we matched each other in height at five feet tall. She meant I would be occupied by tying up my mother's financial affairs, responding to sympathy cards, or become fearful and not return to the place of her death. I didn't believe her. Of course, I would come back soon. I wasn't afraid. I wouldn't stay away.

Beth and I had returned to our mother's room. Slowly, I'd gone through each of her belongings. What should stay? *Love One Another* – a plaque that once had hung over my mother's kitchen and now rested on the ledge over her bed seemed appropriate to leave behind. What should go? Her Sinatra CDs for Janice and Becky, my mother's little black purses which went to my sister Jeanne, and I kept her Christmas caroling dolls.

The task had taken no time. Over the years, I had done my best to scrub the room clean, to save what mattered or replace it with something that stood in for something else. There was little else for me in the room that signified *Mom*. Whatever remained of hers I no longer needed and I left the rest to be donated. Eddie, the maintenance man, had already placed her rocker and nightstand in my car. That day, I walked out with two small cartons and set my sights on packing for my son's college graduation, a duty my mother would have respected.

"It hasn't all been emptied out," Janice said, bringing me back into the conversation at the reception desk.

"I guess there's still clothes in there for other residents that might be of use."

Janice shook her head. "My friend was so small, hard for anyone to fit into her clothes. There's still stuff lying around in there," she said.

It would be hard for Janice to see another woman wearing my mother's clothes, inhabiting the maroon sweater she had once worn with her short arms poking through while pushing on the door to exit into the air that kept her alive, her shirts with gems or rhinestones that reflected light off her cherub face or enhanced her cheeks reddening whenever she was angry or filled with an explosive moment of joy or shame.

I nodded, picked up my purse and pressed the buttons to pass through the second secure door. As I walked down the corridor toward my mother's old room, I looked into each doorway and read all the nameplates—like my mother would have done. Only I was looking for someone missing, and she would have been looking for someone she knew. I said a few quick *hellos* to the residents who were not napping. Miss Betty sat in the same back corner in the same old rocker with the same torn-up acrostic puzzle book she'd been working on for months set on her lap. I was comforted by her sameness in a way I had never been with my mother.

I reached my mother's room, number 13, and slowly entered. The staff really had meant it. My mother's room was not occupied. How many more months would they let her room sit, I wondered, with remnants of her life lying in state across the plastic covering of the bed? For a moment I stood there in the quiet, looking toward the window where she and I had watched the seasons change as we changed too.

"Hi, Mom," I whispered through tears starting to bubble up.

There was a brief silence down the hallway between a rerun of *Gunsmoke* and a commercial for hearing aids.

So I listened, longing for her to whisper back, "Hi, honey." When my mother had been alive, I'd often wondered when she'd called me *honey* if she knew who I was. Desperately, I waited to hear her voice again. She could be angry and I'd be thrilled. Maybe she would call out, "Right there," demanding some ceramic figurine or slip of paper or utility cart be moved. Or, "Get that stupid stuff off down here." And I would rush to do whatever she demanded. I just wanted to hear her voice.

But I heard nothing.

It was time for me to go—and let go.

I returned to the reception area but didn't see Janice or Derek staffing the desk, so I pushed a few buttons on the alarm pad to let myself out, then realized I had forgotten the code. A click came from behind. Someone had pushed the buzzer from the main desk to release me.

When I stepped outside, I could sense winter was coming. Beneath my coat, my arms prickled with goosebumps and the thought of my mother running her hands up and down my arm made the corners of my mouth turn up. The day was darkening overhead, but in the western sky, there was a fissure of light causing a harsh glare. As I pulled out my sunglasses, my mother's voice rang through my head, and I thought I heard, "There you are 'Net. I knew it was you."

259

Acknowledgements

This book would not have been possible without the courage of one executive director, Jana Miller, who approached me weeks after my mother's death, and said, "We think your blog has value for the families and loved ones of those experiencing dementia." Thank you to Jana and to her marketing staff who encouraged me. From there, the project grew from a blog into this book.

Thank you to Janice and Becky. Both women were special to my mother. They were and still are special to me. I hope our friendship outlasts our memories. And to Bobbi, for Baby Doll, for picking up the pieces while I traveled, and for redefining family.

And a special thanks to the caregivers of Arden Courts. Within those four walls of my mother's care home, Mom never experienced dementia and her caregivers never acted as if she did. She was just Jean, or Jean the Bean, or Miss Jean or My Friend. From all of them, I learned how to be with my mother, how to be present with her, to love who she was and who she was becoming. I learned so much by modeling them. Their arms were exactly what my mother needed to hold, and their love was what she needed to live.

To those working out front and behind the scenes to raise awareness of and support individuals with Alzheimer's and other dementias, thank you for your endurance and your openness in creating new paths to loving and caring for those who have been afflicted.

Thank you to my siblings for being present, especially when I was absent. Mom knew you and relished in your warmth and love. To Jeanne and Paul, for keeping a steady, loving watch over Mom and Dad in Amherst the years before they moved. Beth, for the purple folder handoff. For being the Cincinnati safety net for Mom and Dad. Now, we can both travel without worry. Laura, for the cookies you always sent to Mom. And to my nephews and nieces, especially Gia and Sophia. They are from a long line of strong women who will always be there for one another.

To Elaine Olund, my graphic designer, who grasped quickly the importance of cookies in this story. She understood it was one of the few activities, where we as children are side by side with our parents, especially our mothers. And to Lauren Whaley, who kept my words—and me—collected. She wove so many pieces together to create the whole.

To Claudia Reilly, who held court on Thursdays at her home with a spread of cheese and apples, and that one time, a bottle of wine while she and I waited out the thunderstorms. She offered shelter to me that day, and on so many others. When I didn't think my words made sense or I couldn't see how they all came together, she felt and saw the sunshine before it broke through the clouds. She knew it was there all along.

Thank you to my all writing friends, but especially Eva Lewandowski, Ellen Austin-Li, Dee Wiley, Claudia Reilly, Elaine Olund and Paula Kutcher, Michelle Dunford, Tina Neyer, and the community of Women Writing for (a) Change. My mother's life cast a long shadow over mine that I am just now stepping out of and I thank them for welcoming me back into my own light.

To my dog Enzo, who tried—with all his heart—to outlast his heart condition. I mourned him as much as Mom because they both needed my care and that tore my own heart open. A bad day with Mom was always made better by Enzo's deep, loving eyes and warm breath.

Thank you to Cheryl, Chris, Shannon, Kaitlyn and Davis—*Nana's snuggler*—for the times each of them loved my mother, sat with her at the dinner table, laughed with her and not at her, even when she ate the half-wheel of brie or bit into the plastic baby Jesus. They thereby loved me, knowing I will become my mother some day.

To my husband Mark, for the countless hours I left him behind to "go see Mom" and the countless hours he spent as our go-between and coaxing my mother inside where it was warm. He knows who he was to her. He knows who he is to me.

And to Dad/Papu/Ette, whom I can finally mourn. Many months after my mother passed away, I dreamt of him. It was a dream about pansies blooming in his backyard and how hardy they were. And how the pansies grew outside the shade of the tree—the family tree. I learned this: He has forgiven me, I have forgiven myself for not being able to grieve his loss while I moved Mom forward without him. I owe him a debt of gratitude because I doubted him, I doubted myself. He believed in me. His final offering pushed me to love Mom more than I thought possible. My father, the storyteller, will have his own story that I will write someday. I promise it here.

And with love, I thank my mother Vincenzella Jean Giuliani Januzzi. For showing up every damn time. I am thankful I was given the gift of not only her care, but the opportunity to look back on her life. I remember the times when I was a teen, she and I would fight, and I would pout and stomp off to my yellow room. She always gave in first, knocked on my door, sat at the edge of my bed and apologized. She was always the bigger person—though she shrank before my eyes—but not before I could hold all of her in my heart.

Questions for Discussion

1. In *I'll Have Some of Yours*, Annette Januzzi Wick highlights cookies, music, and going outdoors as being essential not only to her mother's well-being, but to their relationship. As a caregiver, what do you think is most important to help someone you love and how do you arrive at that conclusion?

2. Throughout the book, readers see Annette pushing her mother to go for a drive, to exercise, to eat better and "do more." Is that reasonable? Do you feel there are certain things you try to get your loved one to do that the person does not want to do? How do you cope with wanting to help maintain the best quality of life for a loved one, and also feeling let down?

3. How would you describe the relationship between mother and daughter prior to Annette's mother experiencing dementia? How does that change? And why?

4. Imagine a loved one in a situation of losing his or her spouse, and also experiencing memory loss. What are ways in which the caregiver can help with this transition?

5. In a care home, there are many variables that contribute to the success of a loved one settling into a place of peace. How did the author handle this? What are some actions she took to ensure her mother was comfortable? What other things can caregivers do to ensure the same for their loved one?

6. What musical memories do you associate with significant moments in your own life or that of a loved one? How can you use them to deepen your relationships with others or to find peace within yourself?

7. In the end, the author experiences several inspirational moments in her mother's dying. How does what you do now lead to moments similar to those of the author?

Resources

Alzheimer's Association – The Alzheimer's Association is the leading voluntary health organization in Alzheimer's care, support and research. Their mission is to eliminate Alzheimer's disease through the advancement of research; to provide and enhance care and support for all affected; and to reduce the risk of dementia through the promotion of brain health. *www.alz.org*

Arden Courts Memory Care Community – A part of the family of Promedica and HCR-Manorcare communities. *www.arden-courts.org*

Alive Inside: A Story of Music and Memory – *www.aliveinside.us*

Alive Inside Foundation – Helping communities connect - intergenerationally, musically, and empathetically. *www.aliveinside.org*

Cheering for Charity – Enhancing the quality of life for nursing home residents and their families impacted by Alzheimer's and other dementias. *www.cheeringforcharity.org*

Caregiver Action Network – A leading family caregiver organization working to improve the quality of life for the more than 90 million Americans who care for loved ones with chronic conditions, disabilities, disease, or the frailties of old age. *www.caregiveraction.org*

Caregiving.com – Featuring blogs of family caregivers, weekly words of comforts, daily chats, podcasts and free webinars, holding one of the largest online libraries of caregiving stories. Host of the National Caregivers Conference, held each year in November. *www.caregiving.com*

The Gilster Group – Dementia Care Expertise for Healthcare Providers *www.dementiaexperts.com*

Dementia Inclusive Cincinnati – Many communities are coming together to make their cities and public spaces a place where those who are afflicted with dementia or other cognitive challenges still find purpose in their lives and therefore experience a greater sense of belonging. *www.dementiainclusivecincinnati.org*

About the Author

Annette Januzzi Wick grew up in northern Ohio. She graduated from the University of Akron with a Computer Science degree yet still sighs when her cell phone doesn't work. For a time, she made her home in the Pacific Northwest until firmly planting her feet in Cincinnati. When she's not writing, she is walking Cincinnati's fifty-two neighborhoods or finding and making connections in the

OCTOBER - 1967

community. *I'll Have Some of Yours* is based on her award-winning blog, Find You in the Sun (*www.findyouinthesun.com*), where additional essays appear.

Her writings have appeared in the *Alzheimer's Association's Cornerstone, Erma Bombeck Humor Blog, Grief Becomes You: A Narrative of Loss,* and *Movers and Makers*, and have received awards from *Writer's Digest, National Society of Newspaper Columnists, Sinclair College*, and *USA Book News*.

Annette is available for speaking events, book signings and writing workshops. Visit *annettejwick.com* to purchase her book or learn more. *I'll Have Some of Yours* is also available for order through Amazon and major distributors.

Other Books by this Author

I'll Be In the Car: One Woman's Story of Love, Loss and Reclaiming Life

Made in the USA
Monee, IL
14 November 2019